FAITH MISGUIDED
*Exposing the Dangers
of Mysticism*

FAITH MISGUIDED

Exposing the Dangers of Mysticism

ARTHUR L. JOHNSON

MOODY PRESS

CHICAGO

© 1988 by
THE MOODY BIBLE INSTITUTE
OF CHICAGO

Unless otherwise noted, all Scripture quotations are from the *New American Standard Bible,* © 1960, 1962, 1963, 1968, 1971, 1972, 1973, 1975, and 1977 by The Lockman Foundation, and are used by permission.

Library of Congress Cataloging in Publication Data

Johnson, Arthur L., 1935-
      Faith misguided / by Arthur L. Johnson.
            p.   cm.
      ISBN 0-8024-5643-X
      1. Mysticism—Controversial literature.   2. Spirituality—History of doctrines—20th century.   3. Evangelicalism.   I. Title.
      BV5082.2.J6   1988
      248.2'2—dc19   88-807
                                                                            CIP

1 2 3 4 5 6 Printing/BC/Year 92 91 90 89 88

Printed in the United States of America

To my mother, who taught by example that
love for God and love of the truth go hand in hand

CONTENTS

FOREWORD

A mystical maze has settled on our land. Fuzzy thinking is the order of the day. The Good Ship Evangelicalism is sailing without rational rudders in the hazy sea of subjectivity. Into this fog Arthur Johnson's book comes as a beacon in the night. It is a call for sanity and rationality in a day that has largely forgotten both.

There are a number of movements whose combined force in our day has necessitated this call back to reality. European existentialism, Eastern mysticism, evangelical pietism, charismatic enthusiasm, and American pragmatism have all contributed to this flood of experientialism. Many are being swallowed up by Eastern mysticism via the New Age movement. But even Christians who have not forsaken the theistic God of the Bible for the pantheistic God of the East are losing their bearings. Many have lost the God of their experience in their quest for an experience with God. Fact has been replaced by feeling. Truth is measured by subjective experience, not by objective reality.

In the midst of this new wave of subjectivism, Dr. Johnson has provided a clear analysis of the problem and a balanced biblical alternative. " 'Come now, let us reason together,' says the Lord" (Isa. 1:18). "Test the Spirits" (1 John 4:1). "Give an account for the hope that is in you" (1 Pet. 3:15). "Love the Lord with all ... your mind" (Matt. 22:37). "Whatever is true ... let your mind dwell on these things" (Phil. 4:8). These are not idle suggestions; they are biblical imperatives whose value is becoming more apparent day by day. The time is ripe for a book like this. Indeed, it is overdue. Christianity is an appeal to the heart, but God never bypasses the head on the way to the heart. The Scriptures do not oppose feeling as a means of expressing truth (cf. Ps. 150:4-5), but feelings are a notoriously unreliable means for testing truth. Martin Luther saw the issue clearly when he wrote:

> For feelings come and feelings go,
> And feelings are deceiving;
> My warrant is the Word of God,
> Naught else is worth believing.

NORMAN L. GEISLER

PREFACE

At a time when the entire world seems to be turning away from using rational understanding toward a reliance on mystical means as the basis for life, Christians seem unaware of the implications of this trend for the faith. Mysticism, if my understanding of the Bible and of history are correct, is both anti-Scriptural and a contradiction of the evangelical view that the Bible is the one and only ultimate criterion of truth about God and our relation to Him. It is my prayer that this book will be used of God to warn of the danger and to turn many back to seeking an accurate understanding of the Word of God and ot its place in our lives.

I would like to express my deep appreciation to the many who have had a hand in bringing this book to completion. In preparing a work such as this it is always an asset to be on the campus of a university and have the resources of its library available. Library personnel have given assistance for which I am thankful. Organized research funds made the purchase of some books possible and provided released time for research. But individual friends are always the most important component in a work like this. Those who have willingly discussed the issues, made suggestions, encouraged me, and read parts or all of the manuscript, are far too many to mention.

However, a few people have played such a significant role that I must express special thanks to them. Rev. Mike Bellah, has been a friend, counselor, and an encourager. Malcolm and Ann Hughes have critically evaluated and helped sharpen my focus. Norman Geisler has given many beneficial suggestions. Then there is my family. My sons, Brad and Randy, have both contributed a special kind of encouragement, and at times, critical insight. Above all, my wife, Marilyn, has been my friend, loving critic, and long-suffering support. To them all I express deep thanks.

INTRODUCTION

If we were seeking an appropriate label to describe the religious scene in the last three decades of the twentieth century, we would do well to consider it "the age of confusion." There are many different religions in the Western world, each seeking adherents. They range from traditional Christian groups to oriental religions, from spiritist and occult movements to more traditional Western cults. Within each of these there is a confusion of voices, each claiming to speak for the larger group. Rarely can the casual observer detect any clear agreement between these self-proclaimed leaders.

One wishes he could say that this same confusion did not exist in the evangelical community. After all, do not evangelicals agree that the Bible is the authority in doctrinal matters? Surely here we can find agreement and avoid the confusion that permeates the larger religious world around us. We could hope that such confusion would not exist, but unfortunately it does. Here also it seems that "every man [says] that which seems right in his own eyes" (Judg. 21:25b, paraphrased). True, there

13

are areas of general agreement, some of them very important areas. But even here the agreement is often hidden in the confusion of differing terms. Sometimes what seems to be agreement is, after careful examination, not what first appearances would lead one to think.

A Focus Within Religious Confusion

No doubt there are many reasons for this confusion. However, I believe the major sources can be grouped under three interrelated problems: poor scholarship, biblical ignorance, and adherence to nonbiblical philosophical positions. Such philosophical positions often go unrecognized by the person holding them, but they nevertheless function as the criteria by which Scripture is interpreted. To help us clarify our thinking and avoid resultant problems, much needs to be said about each of these reasons. However, the topic of this book concerns the problems that result from accepting a non-biblical philosophical position. Even this is not a completely accurate statement. Rather, it is about the problems arising from accepting only one kind of non-Christian philosophy, namely mysticism.

These three causes of confusion are interrelated. Consequently, the examination of one of them will, to some degree, involve us in the examination of the other two. When evangelicals are guilty of interpreting the Bible and of developing doctrine under the influence of secular philosophies, they generally do so out of ignorance and poor biblical scholarship. As evangelicals, we must construct our philosophical structures in accordance with Scripture. This is part of what we mean when we claim the Bible as our final standard of truth.

No matter how good our intentions may be, when we fail in Scripture interpretation the results are tragic. Our ignorance of basic biblical structures leaves us open to the ever-present influence of the world's thought patterns. When we begin to interpret the Word of God through these patterns, we inevitably distort it. Such distortion is always destructive (2 Pet. 3:16). Some of the resultant problems for the church are our concern here.

A Subtlety in Religious Confusion

Some special problems will face us as we attempt to understand today's religious confusion. These are problems that are unique among the other major difficulties facing Christians today. This is because the distortions caused by mysticism have gained a great deal of respectability within the evangelical community. This, in turn, is partly due to a basic misunderstanding of what the Scriptures mean when they speak of being "spiritual."

Much of what has been taught about spirituality in general, and about the "deeper spiritual life" specifically, has its roots more deeply in medieval Catholic mysticism, and in the mystical experiences of more recent persons, than it has in Scripture. Being convinced by their own experiences that a mystical approach is valid, these persons have interpreted Scripture to fit. This often gives a meaning to the written Word that may be nearly the opposite to that intended by the Holy Spirit. Although much of this has been done by well-intentioned persons, the result has, nevertheless, been tragic in many cases. Often Christians, finding themselves unable to meet the criteria set for them by these writers and speakers, carry a load of totally unjustified guilt. Some despair of ever meeting what they have been taught is God's will for them. Others spend years in fruitless effort that should have been spent in profitable service. These are the results of the more mild forms of the error. More extreme cases have resulted in heresy and, sometimes, in powerful anti-Christian cults. The problem is not an unimportant one.

At the same time, we mostly fail to meet the challenge from the modern secular world. Our failure is because, at least in large part, we are confused about what is the real heart of the issue. Young people who claim to be sincere Christians are attracted to cults of various kinds. Christian leaders find themselves unable "to give a logical defense" of the hope that is in us (1 Pet. 3:15, Amp.*). When they do attempt to deal with the problem, they find themselves lost in a confusion of ideas they do not understand and, therefore, cannot handle adequately. The result is that their efforts are largely unsuccessful. They have been led to believe that a mystical approach is a legitimate aspect of true spirituality. Hence, they spend their time and efforts resisting surface errors in beliefs, while encouraging the very mysticism that is the root of the problem.

I do not mean for a moment that false doctrines and practices should not be opposed. Quite the opposite. They must be resisted and exposed for what they are. If anything, we should probably do so with more vigor and wisdom than we now do. The problem, however, is that if this is all we do we fail in two ways. First, we fail to get at the root of the problem. If the false doctrine springs from mysticism, it will likely be replaced by another error. Second, we often fail to understand correctly the error itself because the key issues are themselves not always what they appear to be. In that case, when we have done all we can, the root error is as strong as ever. We may actually have encouraged the mysticism that is its basis. We have failed!

A Challenge to Religious Confusion

By now someone will be asking, "Just what is this thing you call *mysticism*? Can you support your charge

---

Amplified New Testament.

that evangelical Christianity looks with favor on forms of mysticism that are dangerous?'' These are fair questions and present a valid challenge. I believe that the answer to the second will become clearer once we answer the first in chapter 1. Then, most of the following chapters will be dedicated to showing that the evangelical community today faces grave dangers from mysticism.

However, we will face something of a problem as we try to understand clearly just what mysticism is. No adequate vocabulary exists to define mysticism. Perhaps this helps explain why we have been so little aware of this issue.

Furthermore, the expressions of mysticism with which we are most concerned are rarely encountered in a pure form. What we most often see are attitudes and beliefs that result from what we may describe as low-grade mystical experiences. They are experiences that have the basic characteristics of all mystical experiences, but in a very mild form. Occasionally they share some, but not all, of the essential mystical characteristics. Whether such low-grade experiences should properly be called mystical at all is not our concern here. In the absence of a better term, *mystical* will serve our purposes. What is vital is that we recognize the implications of accepting such experiences as having validity and authority.

Let us begin by examining the pure mystical experience in order to see the problem clearly. Then applications to less dramatic cases can follow.

1
THE NATURE OF MYSTICISM:
Innerness of Reality

The word *mysticism* has never had a precise meaning, and in recent years it has been used in so many different ways that most people now have no clear idea of what it means. It is, however, the best word available in spite of its weaknesses. Consequently, before we can profitably discuss how mysticism relates to Christian truth and practice, we need to define the term.

GENERAL DESCRIPTION OF MYSTICAL INNERNESS

It is much easier to explain what I do *not* mean by mysticism. First, I do not mean that confusion of beliefs and practices that we call "the occult," even though there often is much of the mystical in the occult.

Another meaning that must be rejected is that which many adherents to the philosophy of naturalism give to the word. For them, *mystical* and *supernatural* are often used synonymously. Some mystics deny that their mysticism involves anything supernatural at all, although this group seems to be quite small. Most claim that when they are in a mystical trance they are in contact with the supernatural, but this alone is not what is meant by mysticism.

Others seem to equate mysticism totally with Oriental religions. This is also wrong, for although the major oriental religions such as Hinduism, Buddhism, and Taoism are mystical, there has been a strong mystical element in certain Western religions and philosophies as well.

Finally, mysticism must not be confused with *mystery*, even though the words are related historically. To call something mystical is not to say that it is hidden, or difficult, or impossible to understand. The meaning is quite different from any of these.

There are two aspects to mysticism that we must recognize to avoid confusion. First, there is a psychological aspect, often called the mystical experience. Then there are the beliefs that arise from that experience. These philosophical and religious beliefs constitute a set of ideas sometimes collectively called *mysticism*. However, the term *mysticism* is often used for both the experience itself and the beliefs resulting from it. Our first major concern is to answer the question, What makes an experience mystical?

When we speak of a mystical experience we refer to an event that is completely within the person. It is totally subjective. When I describe it as being "inner," and on occasions as "private," I have the same thing in mind. Although the mystic may experience it as having been triggered by occurrences or objects outside himself (like a sunset, a piece of music, a religious ceremony, or even a sex act),[1] the mystical experience is a totally inner event. It contains no essential aspects that exist externally to him in the physical world. Some examples may help to make this a bit clearer.

1. Andrew M. Greeley, *Ecstasy, A Way of Knowing* (Englewood Cliffs, N.J.: Prentice Hall, 1974), p. 92.

Andrew M. Greeley relates the following as an example of the kind of event we are discussing.

> A troubled young man has been listening to Beethoven's Ninth Symphony on a phonograph in his apartment. He turns off the music and begins to work on a term paper, but he makes little progress. The doubts, the fears, the thoughts of self-destruction that have harassed him before return. Then, in counterpoint, he hears the hymn of the Ode to Joy, and something, perhaps someone, takes possession of the room and of him. The doubts, the fears, the anxieties are dispelled forever; the young man *knows* there is nothing to worry about.[2]

It may be useful to notice that Greeley tells us something about this young man's state of mind before the experience as well as after, but little about the experience itself. We are told that he "hears the hymn of the Ode to Joy" yet, we are told, he had already turned off the music. This "hearing" of part of the Ninth Symphony apparently has no actual physical basis. What are we to make of the statement that "something, perhaps someone, takes possession of the room and of him"? We are probably to understand that this is how the young man felt. The key concept Greeley seems to wish to communicate is that which he emphasizes in the last line of the description. He says that the feeling of confidence and well-being is so strong that it completely convinces the young man that everything is all right. Greeley insists this is properly called "knowing." The change in the young man's conviction about his condition is not based on any change in the outside world or on any objective facts. The entire event occurred within the young man himself.

Later in this same book Greeley makes a claim, which one hears not infrequently, that the Bible is full of

2. Ibid., p. 2.

mystical experiences. As evidence, he points to Paul's experience on the road to Damascus.[3] This, however, is wrong. Paul tells us that there was a light and a voice. In Acts 9:7 we are told that those who were with Paul also heard the voice, although they did not understand what was said. In Acts 22:9 they also saw the light. Unless we reject the accuracy of the account, the Damascus Road experience consisted of a series of objective events. These events occurred "out in the open" where they were shared by all those present and were, therefore, not purely subjective or confined to Paul's mind.

Another biblical event that is wrongly called a mystical experience is Moses' encounter with God at the burning bush. If we accept the accuracy of the record, this was not a mystical experience because there really was a bush, it was really on fire, and the voice of God actually spoke audibly to Moses. These were public events—that is, events in the real world, rather than imaginary occurrences. If there had been other people present, they also could have heard the voice and seen the bush burning.[4]

In the way we are using the term, then, an experience cannot be called mystical if it consists of events in the objective, public world, although such objective events might happen to be what triggered the experience. However, we should be quick to add that the mystic may perceive his subjective events as being in his surroundings. He may believe the event occurred in the objective world, but other people with him did not sense it and could not have done so. Generally, however, the mystic realizes the things he experiences are not objective.

3. Ibid., p. 136.
4. I can find no events described in the Bible that are undisputably mystical experiences. There are, however, a few that might qualify, although we are given too little information ever to be absolutely certain, in my judgment. One of these is Paul's description of "a man . . . caught up to the third heaven" (2 Cor. 12:1-5).

By now it is likely apparent that what we describe as a mystical experience is primarily an emotive event, rather than a cognitive one. By this I mean that its predominant qualities have more to do with emotional intensity, or "feeling tone," than with facts evaluated and understood rationally. Although this is true, it alone is a woefully inadequate way of describing the mystical experience. The force of the experience is often so overwhelming that the person having it finds his entire life changed by it. Mere emotions cannot effect such transformations.

Furthermore, it is from this emotional quality that another characteristic results, namely, its "self-authenticating" nature. The mystic rarely questions the goodness and value of his experience. Consequently, if he describes it as giving him information, he rarely questions the truth of his newly gained "knowledge."[5] It is this claim that mystical experiences are "ways of knowing" truth that is vital to understanding many religious movements we see today.

On the other hand, to speak of "emotional intensity" is debatable. Many, if not most, mystics would say that what they experience is not emotional at all. In fact, they often insist that the dominant quality of the experience is the total absence of all emotion or sensation. However, if we draw a broad distinction between intellectual activity, on the one hand, and emotional experiences on the other; and if we then force all that we experience into one category or the other; then mystical experience must be called "emotional" rather than "intellectual" or "cognitive." This bifurcation of human experience is exceedingly simplistic, but I believe it will help as we attempt to grasp what we mean by mystical experience.

5. Edgar D. Mitchell, *Psychic Exploration* (New York: Putnam's, 1974), p. 613. See also Greeley, p. 4.

The way I have attempted to describe the mystical experience may lead some to think I am suggesting that such an occurrence is a case of conscious self-delusion and is, therefore, completely in the control of the mystic. According to practitioners, however, this is not true. They say that mystical experiences cannot be easily induced. Some mystics claim they cannot ever be induced. Many mystics report that these experiences catch them completely by surprise. Others believe that one can prepare himself for them. In fact, yoga is a practice intended to be such a preparation. Drug use, as a religious act, is seen as a way of inducing mystical trances, but many mystics see drug states as counterfeit mystical experiences. Some mystics believe long periods of preparation are necessary before significant experiences may be expected.[6]

Thus far I have been trying to describe the mystical experience itself. I have said it is a psychological experience, totally within the person, having an emotional tone, and that it often has a life-changing intensity about it that sets it off from other experiences. I have also said that the experience proper is totally subjective, and therefore is not open to others. This last aspect requires further examination.

Although, I suppose, two or more people might have mystical experiences at the same time that were triggered by the same external events, there is no basis for saying they were having the same mystical experience. This observation is, of course, not unique to mystical experi-

6. William James, *The Varieties of Religious Experience* (New York: Macmillan, 1961), pp. 315-18. James's discussion of this issue was strongly supported by my own experience. I studied Oriental religions for some months under a man trained as a Buddhist monk. He vehemently rejected drug experiences, saying that he had tried them and they produced only a counterfeit mystical experience. True experiences resulted only from long preparation through yoga, he insisted.

ences. If you and I both have a toothache, I have no right to say we are having the same experience, except to mean we are having experiences we believe to be similar. My experience of a toothache is not your experience of a toothache. I can never "get into your skin" and feel your pain. Pain is private in a way that watching a sunset together is not. In the latter case, we believe that we are both seeing the same sunset, even though we may pay attention to different aspects of the event. In the case of pain, we know we are not experiencing the same pain, although we may believe it to be similar. Even though we may sense the sunset somewhat differently, there are still a great number of the components that are common to us both. In other words, they are objective. In the case of pain, little if anything is common other than the word *pain*. The components of having a toothache are nearly all subjective.

It is the lack of objectivity in the mystical experience that presents the major difficulty for the mystic when he tries to justify his claim to knowledge.

We are now ready to develop a more formal definition of mysticism. It will be helpful to do this from three slightly different perspectives: first, the psychological aspects; second, the philosophical implications; and finally, the theological expressions.

The psychological dimensions involve assigning primary significance to inward, subjective, nonrational impressions. It involves seeing intense, noncognitive, subjective experiences as having such deep significance that they should be sought. One's life should be directed by them.

For many people, mysticism is an unexamined psychological attitude—one that while it may profoundly influence their lives, is not clearly understood and may not even be recognized. But for a knowledgeable mystic who has sought to understand his commitment to the mystic way, this psychological attitude is grounded in a philosophical belief. This belief sees truth and knowledge as attainable through mystical experience. All truth is tested by inner, subjective impressions rather than by its logical consistency or other rational considerations.[7] When mystical states constitute an intense experience, this experience is seen as somehow a "union" with whatever is ultimate, and therefore as the proper fulfillment of human existence.[8]

When either the psychological attitude alone, or the more complete philosophical grasp, is translated into theological terms, the resulting view leads the person to equate his inner impressions or subjective states with the voice of God. Such a person, if he is a Christian, tends to believe that the activity of the Holy Spirit within us is expressed primarily through emotional or other noncognitive aspects of our being. Having and "obeying" such experiences is what "being spiritual" is all about.

RELIGIOUS USE OF MYSTICAL INNERNESS

It is time now to turn our attention from the description of mystical experience to the use of mystical experiences in religious movements of our day. A key point to keep in mind has already been stressed: the claim of the mystic that the mystical experience provides knowledge. A quick look at what is implied by the term *knowledge* may help us here. Two aspects are important. First, to say that I know something is to say not only that I am aware of that something, but also that it is true. If, for example, I

---

7. Watchman Nee, *The Spiritual Man* (New York: Christian Fellowship Publishers, 1968), 2:75-76.
8. William Ralph Inge, *Mysticism in Religion* (Westport, Conn.: Greenwood, 1948), p. 25. See also W. T. Stace, *Mysticism and Philosophy* (London: Macmillan, 1960), p. 66.

say that I know that the earth is flat, I am also saying (false-ly) that it is true that the earth is flat, and that I am aware that this is so.

The second use of the term *knowledge* relates most clearly to people. If I say that I know Harry, I am saying that I am experientially acquainted with him. Some have occasionally implied that one can know a person without knowing any facts about him. But this is false. Truly to know a person, one must be aware of some accurate information about him, as well as being experientially acquainted with him. This is important in our study, because one cannot say one knows God without knowing some accurate information about Him.

The mystic claims to gain knowledge in both of the senses we have described. He believes he gains truth about something ultimate and that he also becomes experientially acquainted with whatever that ultimate reality is. The first kind of knowledge is described by William James under what he calls the "noetic quality" of mystical experiences.

> Although so similar to states of feeling, mystical states seem to those who experience them to be also states of knowledge. They are states of insight into depths of truth unplumbed by the discursive intellect. They are illuminations, revelations, full of significance and importance, all inarticulate though they remain; and as a rule they carry with them a curious sense of authority for aftertime.[9]

It seems that for some, this "sense of authority" is so compelling that they insist that there is no possibility that they are mistaken in what they have come to believe. It is this compelling sense of the truth that I refer to as the

9. William James, p. 300.

self-authenticating nature of the mystical experience. It is from these "noetic qualities" that much of the theology of the new religions is derived.

A further curious aspect related to the noetic quality of the experience is the argument one often encounters when challenging a mystic. He may argue that since the non-mystic has not had the experience he has had, the non-mystic is therefore not qualified to sit in judgment on it. One often hears the claim that "I just know," with a refusal to further discuss or defend the issue.

If we ask the religious mystic what the source of this claimed knowledge is, and what it is knowledge of, he will answer that it is knowledge of God, or of some aspect of His will, and that its source is God Himself.[10] In other words, the mystic claims, either openly or by implication, that God has revealed Himself to the mystic, or else He has revealed some new, vital information. If it was God's self-revelation, doctrine can be developed from it. Otherwise, the teaching itself is said to be directly from God. Either way, the religious mystic claims to have experienced God and to have received special revelations.

How are we to react to the mystic's claims? A series of rather significant issues must be confronted if evangelical Christians are to see their way clearly in dealing with these claims.

For convenience I will divide these issues into two groups. First, there are problems that result from the actual phenomenon of mysticism. These difficulties are theoretical, but they are also significant for the evangelical Christian since they relate directly to certain basic Christian doctrines. Second, there are problems that result from the nature of the revelations the mystic claims to have received. Here the central issue is specific doc-

10. Inge, p. 8.

trines derived from mystical experiences. Among these is the doctrine of God.

It is vitally important that we clearly understand both groups of problems, lest we be caught in that trap that allows us to accept a false principle because the specific application of that principle seems to be legitimate. For example, suppose we find a person who claims to have gained, by means of a mystical experience, a specific bit of information that we happen to know to be true. Does the truth of the information prove that mystical experience is a valid means of gaining knowledge? Of course it does not. The fact that one piece of information is true does not prove that the means by which it was discovered will always (or even usually) provide true information. It may be totally accidental that the mystical experience yields valid information.

The first issues that need to be examined result from the mystic's claim to have gained truth. Two factors, one largely philosophical and the other doctrinal, both closely related, demand consideration. What is the criterion by which we determine truth? Or, stated in other terms, When is a statement true? and, By what standard do we determine that it is true? This is the philosophical issue.

The doctrinal problem grows out of it. Evangelical Christians maintain that the Bible is the only standard for faith and practice—the only and ultimate criterion in all matters concerning our spiritual life (2 Pet. 1:2-4; 2 Tim. 3:16).[11] If this is so, is there any place for such extrabiblical sources of knowledge as mystical experiences in the Christian's life?

A closely related issue concerns whether or not God's special revelation to man is complete in the Scrip-

11. Lewis Sperry Chafer, *Systematic Theology* (Dallas: Dallas Seminary Press, 1947), 1:15.

tures. Most Protestant Christians, until recently, have always believed and taught that it is. While there is no Scriptural passage that explicitly states this, Biblical scholars have long maintained that there is strong implicit evidence in the Word that direct revelation was to cease with the death of those who were eye-witnesses of Christ's life, death, and resurrection. It seems quite significant that most, if not all, claims to direct revelations made by self-proclaimed prophets since the close of the canon have resulted in serious problems for the church. They have also been the source of many major heresies.[12]

If God's special revelation to man is complete in the Scripture, then the mystic's claim to direct revelation must be rejected. This applies not only when it conflicts with biblical teaching, but also when it claims to be in line with the Word but goes beyond what the Bible teaches. All that we need to know is either already directly contained in the written Word or is implied by what it says; or else it is revealed in and through God's general revelation, His creation. To claim a further revelation is to deny the sufficiency and completeness of what has already been given.

If, however, a supposed revelation neither conflicts with, nor adds to, what is already revealed, it is then no real revelation. This is so because nothing is being revealed that is not already known, and there is no need for it. Thus, in either case, a claim to new revelation must be rejected, either as conflicting with God's Word or as be-

12. Consider, for example, the tragic results of the claims to direct revelation made by some members of the radical wing of the Anabaptist movement. Although there were many specific instances during that period of history, the incident at the city of Munster was especially tragic. On the basis of supposed revelations from God, both private property and monogamous marriage was abolished. The incident finally culminated in the massacre of many of the defenders of the city and the torture of others (Williston Walker, *The Reformation*, vol. 9 of *Ten Epochs of Church History*, ed. John Fulton [New York: Scribners, 1900], pp. 342-44.) For further validation of this claim, one need only examine the history of modern cults.

ing superfluous. But such a "revelation" is never *only* superfluous, because if accepted as a revelation it makes legitimate the claim that new, special revelations are possible, and therefore potentially valid.

The evangelical Christian, then, must reject the mystic's claim to direct revelation from God for several reasons, some of which we will examine later. But at this point, he must do so primarily because it, in effect, results in the position that there is at least one other way, beside through Scripture, of gaining knowledge of God.

Thus far we have been discussing the doctrinal issues. We must also understand what it means when we say that the Scriptures are the final criterion of truth. The Christian's response to the philosophical question is that in matters relating to spiritual issues, the Bible is the final criterion of truth and the standard by which truthclaims are tested in other areas as well. The mystic, however, proposes another criterion, although this is generally done more by implication and practice than by explicit statement. For him, inner, nonrational experience is the ultimate criterion.[13] There is something about the experience that sets it apart, putting it above question. In some cases, the intensity of the experience seems to be what makes it self-authenticating. The experience convinces the mystic in such a way, and to such a degree, that he simply cannot doubt its value and the correctness of what he believes it "says."[14]

13. Inge, pp. 9, 22. An interesting, but tragic, sidelight to all this is that although he was formerly a clergyman in the Anglican church and held a high position in that body, Inge openly rejects the authority of the Scripture. He calls it "a broken reed" (p. 20) and says that it is "hopelessly discredited, except in low intellectual strata" (p. 18). He wished to maintain that mystical experience is the only adequate source of knowledge about God.

14. My point here is not that he is forced to believe it in such a way that we can say that he actually could not help himself. Rather, given his personality, beliefs, state of ignorance, and so forth, he sees his experience as totally convincing and sees no possibility that it might be false.

However, another element of quite recent origin seems prevalent in at least some cases. In its crudest form this position says that believing something to be so makes it so.[15] The idea is that ultimate reality is purely mental; therefore one is able to create whatever reality one wishes. Thus the mystic "creates" truth through his experience. In a less extreme form, the view seems to be that there are "alternate realities," one as real as another, and that these "break in upon" the mystic in his experiences. Whatever form is taken, the criterion of truth is again a purely private and subjective experience that provides no means of verification and no safeguard against error. Nevertheless, it is seen by the mystic as being above question by others.

The practical result of all this is that it is nearly impossible to reason with any convinced mystic. Such people are generally beyond the reach of reason. However, those in the process of being drawn into mystical movements can often be made aware of the irrational and questionable nature of what they are being asked to believe. Sensitivity to these issues by Christian leaders is vital today if we are to "guard . . . the flock . . . the church of God" (Acts 20:28-31), as Paul urged the leaders of the church. I am convinced that many evangelicals, especially young people, who are in more direct contact with the mystical elements of our society, would be spared much spiritual danger if their leaders were themselves better prepared to recognize, analyze, and evaluate these elements, and then alert the people. Ignorance of mysticism and the issues that accompany it in today's world is a serious danger.

15. For a good discussion of this issue, see James W. Sire, *The Universe Next Door* (Downers Grove, Ill.: Inter-Varsity, 1976), pp. 178-83.

TRUTH CLAIMS OF MYSTICAL INNERNESS

We must be cautious as we turn to some of the problems that result from the nature of the alleged "revelations" mystics claim to receive. Ultimately each mystic's views are unique and must be examined individually, because there is much diversity. In fairness, we must not assume that what is true of one is necessarily true of all. However, certain common tendencies exist.

It seems that the mystical experience often involves a feeling of "union" or "oneness" with either the totality of the universe or some aspect of it.[16] For the mystic whose background is Christian and who brings with him some knowledge of Christian theology and a conviction of its truth, this may take the form of a feeling of "union with God."[17] Precisely what that means may vary from person to person. The description may range from that of an experience of the "indwelling Christ" to a declaration that one is in some sense "becoming God."

An article in the magazine *Catholic Charismatic* used such terms as "we feel *one* with God" (italics the author's), ". . . God as immanently present within us, drawing us into a union of His being with our being . . . ," and, ". . . energies of God divinizing them into children of God. . . ."[18] Precisely what the author intended to convey by such terms as "immanently present," "union," "one with God," and "divinizing" is difficult to say, but a straightforward reading of them seems to say that the mystic either is God or is becoming God is some sense. However, the biblical position never blurs the separate-

---

16. James, p. 329. See also Evelyn Underhill's definition of mysticism as "the art of union with Reality" in *Practical Mysticism* (New York: Dutton, 1943), p. 3.
17. Stace, p. 34.
18. George A. Maloney, S. J., "Mysticism and Charismatic Experience," *Catholic Charismatic* 1, no. 1 (March/April 1976): 29,31.

ness between God and man (even redeemed man). Man
was created as man, and he never becomes anything other than man. Christ became man, but man never becomes
God. Many of the mystical trends in modern society,
however, claim either that man is God or is becoming
God.[19] The theme that man becomes God is quite prominent in recent science fiction as well, sometimes mixed
with a clearly occult, mystical element and sometimes
with an evolutionary, naturalistic kind of mysticism.[20]

But even when the results are not as openly contrary
to Christian truth as the foregoing "union," there is still a
serious difficulty. Many mystics come to see the goal of
the spiritual life to be this union—not salvation and
Christian maturity. Mystical union must not be confused
with salvation or anything it involves. The difference between the two, crudely stated, is this: Salvation concerns
what God has done and is doing for and in us, whereas
the mystic's union concerns how he feels. Salvation is
objective (although subjective elements should result),
but union is primarily subjective. This point is illustrated
by Margaret L. Furse in her book *Mysticism: Window on
a World View* when she says, "The great religious motivation of the mystic is to recover the original state of oneness from which we are apparently (though the mystic
assumes not really) separated."[21] To "recover the . . . state
of oneness" that we have not really lost means that we
become aware of our oneness or our identity with something. That is, we are to feel one with something from
which we have really never been separated. This "something," of course, is God, as the context of that quote
makes clear. Thus, Furse is saying that the mystic really

19. Compare the concept of the self in Eastern pantheistic monism with the
    view of the self in New Consciousness as discussed by Sire, pp. 129-203.
20. For one example that expresses this position, see *Jacob Atabet* by Michael
    Murphy (Millbrae, Calif.: Celestial Arts, 1977).
21. Margaret L. Furse, *Mysticism: Window on a World View* (Nashville: Abing-
    don, 1977), p. 15.

does not believe that he is recovering anything objective, but rather he is only recovering his own subjective sense of identity with God.

When the mystic "assumes (we are) not really separated," he is, I take it, denying the reality of the effects of the Fall. Or perhaps rather, he is denying all the effects of the Fall except the feeling of separation from God. This separation is abolished through the mystical experience, not "by grace . . . through faith" (Eph. 2:8) in Christ's finished work on the cross. The objective reality of Christ's sacrifice is unnecessary, as is any knowledge of it, or trust in it. At best, the attention has been shifted from Christ to feelings and inner experiences.

We should recognize another possibility in Furse's description of "the great religious motivation of the mystic." Those who take this attitude hold a position identical to, or very near, that of pantheism. To be identical with God is to say that in some sense we are God. This, of course, is totally contrary to biblical Christianity (2 Thess. 2:3-4).

Again I must add a caution. Many Christians who speak the mystic's language would deny that Christ's sacrifice was unnecessary or that they hold a pantheistic concept of God. But even if they themselves do not believe that Christ's death was unnecessary, the emphasis on the inner subjective experience still has the effect of shifting others' attention from it and from genuine belief. The correctness of my own belief does not give me license to say whatever I please. I am responsible to some degree for what others believe as a result of my statements.

In some mystics, this emphasis on "oneness" and "union" is part of a world view that occasionally seems to result from mystical experience.[22] Briefly, the position is that all reality is ultimately mental in some sense, and

22. Stace, p. 131.

that it is a radical oneness, or whole, in the sense that all distinctions, diversities, qualities, characteristics, and so forth, are illusions and have no basis in fact. Thus, to feel distinct from anything real is a mistake, and therefore, the attempt to regain the feeling of union is an attempt to feel correctly about things. Furthermore, since in their view reality is "in the mind only," feeling correctly is very important.

Because this position is so clearly contrary to common sense and is so different from what most of us take for granted, it is a difficult position for the common person to understand. Still, many people today hold this position, at least to some extent, as a result of giving credence to mystical experiences.

This conviction that all is somehow "one" helps to explain why many mystics have a tendency to deny the difference between good and evil, right and wrong. If all is one in such a way that distinctions cannot be drawn, then obviously the distinction between good and evil cannot really be made. All is really good, and evil is said to be only an illusion. Time is also said to be an illusory distinction. We sense time in discrete moments. This, according to many mystics, is false, since all time is now.[23]

Lawrence LaShan, in a book entitled *The Medium, the Mystic, and the Physicist*, tries to show that the world view within which spiritist mediums operate, and which the mystic experiences, is the same as that of certain theories in advanced physics.[24] He quotes Bertrand Russell as analyzing the claims of mystics under four statements:

23. Bertrand Russell, *Mysticism and Logic* (London: Allen & Unwin, 1963), p. 22ff.
24. Lawrence LaShan, *The Medium, the Mystic, and the Physicist* (New York: Viking, 1974). LaShan's purpose seems to be to provide legitimacy for his own mystical views by arguing that they coincide with those of science —specifically physics.

1. That there is a fundamental unity to all things.
2. That time is an illusion.
3. That all evil is mere appearance.
4. That there is a better way of gaining information than through the senses.

Of these four, the claim that evil is mere appearance is the one that most obviously contradicts the biblical position. The other three, however, are also denials of other aspects of Christian doctrine.

The claim that time is an illusion is the basis for several sorts of strange positions. For example, it is either this position itself, or a closely related one, that is usually found among those who believe in reincarnation. Perhaps even more significantly, a denial of the reality of time allows for a blurring of the line between reality and imagination, and between actual history and myth. This strikes at the basis of the Christian claim that God really entered into human history, that the events associated with Christ's life were actual events, not myths, and that there are certain specific facts that must be believed if we are to meet the demands of a righteous God. When we destroy the distinction between real and imagined events, as the claim that time is an illusion tends to do, one result is that the way is opened to say that truth is whatever one happens to believe. It has no real relation to the objective world of actual events and things. Truth may then be said to be totally subjective and relative.

Something must be said about the fourth claim cited by Russell describing a better way of gaining information than through the senses. Stated in this way, Christians might be tempted to agree. After all, mere sense experience is not an adequate basis for gaining all necessary information. To say that senses alone are adequate is the position of empiricism. This is the epistemological theory of scientific materialism that has been the recent in-

tellectual enemy of evangelical Christianity. But if we see
here only a rejection of empiricism, we miss the really
significant aspects of what the mystic maintains. First,
what is said to be "a better way" is the way of mystical
experience, itself no friend to Christianity.

Of still greater importance, however, is that this
claim is not only a rejection of sense experience but also
a rejection of reason, as a careful examination of mystical
writers will quickly show. By revealing Himself through
the written Word, God has committed Himself to using
rational concepts as a tool for revelation, thereby making
human reason absolutely necessary. This is no mistake,
accident, or afterthought on His part, but an expression of
His perfect will. Yet mystic literature abounds with statements that reject the reasoning ability as an adequate tool
for gaining knowledge. This attitude of rejection ranges
from a mild position that reason is fine for many things
but there is a better way, to the claim that reason always
misleads because it deals only with elements that are un-
real.

One of the more mild statements by a religious mystic is that made by Maloney in the article from which I
quoted earlier, "Mysticism and Charismatic Experience":
"In the superior knowledge in which God communicates
Himself to men more directly and immediately, Christians of deep prayer know, not through concepts, but by
means of direct 'seeing' of God's revelation."[25] Notice
that Maloney is claiming knowledge of God for the mystic through a nonrational, nonconceptual direct "seeing."
"Deep prayer" is his term for a kind of mystical experience, which he argues is an advanced kind of prayer. The
Scriptures are not involved here, though, since he is a
Roman Catholic, I do not suppose he would say that the
Bible is without any importance. The place of conceptual

25. Maloney, pp. 29, 31.

knowledge and the process of reasoning is clearly seen as being, at best, of lesser value than this "direct seeing."

What we have seen thus far may not appear too serious to some. Of much more serious consequence is the rejection of what is known in logic as the law of noncontradiction.[26] This principle states that of any two statements that are actual contradictions, one must be false and the other true. When this principle is rejected by someone, he believes that any statement he makes can be true, even though it directly contradicts some other statement already known to be true. Thus the mystic, rejecting reason but trusting his experiences, can (and often does) believe totally contradictory propositions. Again, the line between truth and falsehood is blurred, and another test of truth is rejected.

We should keep in mind that contemporary society has as one of its most prominent features a strong antirational element, and that the tendency to reject the law of noncontradiction is a major aspect of that anti-rationality.[27] This fact results in two trends that affect the church. First, it makes people much more amenable to false teaching, much less capable of detecting error. Second, it tends to neutralize what has been one of the strong points of the gospel message throughout the centuries: its inherently rational character.[28] Thus, many Chris-

---

26. I would suggest that the reader consult any good textbook on logic. For example, see Irving Copi, *Introduction to Logic* (New York: Macmillan, 1986), pp. 306-7.
27. Francis Schaeffer has repeatedly called attention to this fact. See for example, his little book *Escape from Reason* (Downers Grove, Ill: Inter-Varsity, 1968).
28. The scope of this book will not allow me to develop this theme, and the statement may come as a surprise to some who have come to accept the false claims made by the world that Christianity is irrational. The issue is not whether science, for example, or Christianity is more rational, but rather what set of presuppositions provide the correct starting point for the rational process. Christians claim that God's revelation provides the proper starting point. Scientific naturalism, on the other hand, maintains that such theories as the uniformitarian thesis and empiricism provide the proper starting points. In short, the issue turns on which articles of faith one will accept, not whether one is more rational—that is, whether one or the other follows the rules of correct thought more closely.

tians cannot understand how someone can believe some of the doctrines of the new religious movements, and therefore they fail to take both the claims of the religion and its adherents seriously.

Not only does mysticism have the strong tendency to reject reason and thereby lead to a rejection of a propositional revelation, it also directly endangers another fundamental Christian doctrine. The inclination to see everything as a "oneness" and the trust in subjective feeling often result in a non-Christian concept of God. The tendency is to deny the Trinity in some cases and in others to see God as a force, not a Person. If ultimate reality is a oneness, the mystic reasons, then God must be an absolute unity. The Trinity cannot be understood as consisting of three distinct Persons. At best, the doctrine must be seen as only a convenient way of describing different functions of God.

On the other hand, if God is an absolute oneness, then the concept of personhood seems vastly inappropriate when applied to Him. Personhood is seen as a limiting characteristic and an aspect of diversity. It points to distinctions and differences. Persons are many. Besides, to call God a Person is to draw attention both to His uniqueness from some things and His similarity to others. Hence, many mystics describe God in terms more appropriate to an impersonal force than to a Person, although some may hesitate to say openly that He is only a force. Some are inclined to describe Him only in psychological or emotional terms, such as "Love" or "Light." For others, the tendency is to drift ever nearer to total pantheism.

SUMMARY AND CONCLUSION

It may be well to say a few words by way of clarification and summary. Mysticism, as I have defined it, has as its essential element a certain deep trust in inner, subjective feeling states, which are seen as both good and valuable in themselves and as truth-bearing. Because they are subjective and therefore private to each individual mystic, it is impossible to say if the experiences that any two mystics have are in any significant sense closely similar. Because they are emotive states, they are in a sense ineffable. By this we mean that their essence cannot be put into words just as the taste of an onion, for example, cannot be described accurately and completely to one who has never tasted an onion. The best we can do with mystical states is to identify some very general characteristics, such as that they are intense, that they are often very pleasant, or that they are such that the person having them often finds it hard to doubt their value.

Thus far we have simply described a phenomenon. Our actual concern rests with what is done with these experiences. We are disturbed that mystics exhibit certain tendencies and make certain kinds of claims. I have tried to show that the subjective nature of the mystical experience makes it impossible for the mystic to justify his claims. He cannot show that his experience is an adequate means of gaining information. Nor can he show that the supposed information is true.

I have also argued that the Christian should reject mystical experiences, because God has chosen to relate to man by means of man's mind, not through his emotions. The Word, which must be understood, is the ultimate criterion of truth. Subjective experience is not an adequate basis by which to judge the truth of anything.

When the mystical experience is said to be a revelation from God, this must also be rejected, because the supposed revelation is either superfluous or contrary to the written Word. It is also dangerous because it sets the stage for further "revelations" that may well be false. Accepting mysticism is a rejection of the doctrine of a completed and sufficient revelation in the Scriptures.

Finally, we have examined some false doctrinal positions that have resulted from mystical experiences. Here we should be careful if we wish to be fair. Although many religious mystics hold all these false views, there are some who, no doubt, hold none of them. It is not the believing of certain specific views that makes one a mystic. However, to be a mystic is itself an open door to false doctrine. As a result, I will argue later that the greater danger today for the church does not lie in the false teachings of mystically based cults, as dangerous as these are, but rather in the tendency in the church to confuse the voice of the Holy Spirit with mystical experience. This opens Christians to "every wind of doctrine."

2

THE CHALLENGE OF MYSTICISM:
Infiltration of Evangelicalism

The problems that mysticism presents for the evangelical, Protestant Christian are both unique and critical. They are unique in that mysticism challenges a very fundamental element of evangelicalism in a way it does not do in other religious movements. They are critical because if this challenge is not successfully met evangelicalism will cease to be evangelical. What is being called into question by the mystical approach is the very nature and importance of the Holy Scriptures.

DANGERS OF MYSTICISM'S INFILTRATION

However, these challenges are evidently not apparent to many Christian leaders. Instead, mysticism, presenting itself in the cloak of profound spirituality, so affects many of our most sincere ministers and authors that they unwittingly promote it.

As one might expect, mysticism takes a unique form in evangelical circles. Evangelicals do not generally talk of "union" with God in the way other mystics might. Nor do they openly promote trance states as a means for spiritual growth. Rather, mysticism is promoted as an aspect of the normal, daily Christian life. It is seen as the means for living life in a way that pleases God.

In evangelical circles, perhaps more than in some other groups, the attention has been on the subjective aspects of the Christian life as being of primary significance. For example, when asked to describe their conversion to Christianity, many people say little or nothing about basic beliefs. Rather, they describe the purely subjective aspects of their conversion experiences. The description of how a righteous life is achieved generally centers on psychological dimensions also. The social aspects of godly living are often subordinated to the subjective. In some cases the dominant view appears to be that overt moral behavior is valueless unless certain psychological urges are the root of that action.

This fascination with the subjective has had at least two results: first, the spiritual life is seen primarily in subjective, psychological terms rather than objective, behavioral ones; and second, the goals of prayer, Bible reading, church attendance, and so forth, are thought to be personal, psychological change. Both of these results contain legitimate elements that become objectionable when they assume distorted and imbalanced proportions. Such distortion is likely to occur when Christian concern with the subjective dimension is mentally linked with the world's mystical definition of what it means to be spiritual. The result is evangelical mysticism.

Perhaps the greatest danger for evangelical Christians lies in the way they approach the Scriptures. In their hunger for immediate subjective effects, believers are in peril of treating the Bible merely as a tool for applicational impact, while bypassing foundational interpretation. Much devotional reading of the Scriptures falls into this trap. This is borderline mysticism.

EXAMPLE OF MYSTICISM'S INFILTRATION

"Evangelical mysticism" is unwittingly encouraged by certain ways of explaining Scripture—ways that seem harmless enough on the surface, but that may prove to be very misleading. Often these have been sanctified by long use, but have little real biblical basis. One such case, for example, involves drawing a distinction between two kinds of so-called knowledge, "head knowledge" and "heart knowledge."

Now it should be pointed out that not everyone who speaks of "heart knowledge" has a mystical "knowing" in mind. Often one simply means that cognitive information must be received and applied to be of spiritual value. This, of course, is true. The writer of the book of James makes that amply clear (James 2:14-26). If all that was ever meant by speaking of "heart knowledge" was that we must act on what we know, then there would be no objection to the expression. Unfortunately, all too often this is neither the intended nor the understood meaning.

Rather, what is implied is that there are two distinctly different kinds of knowing, one that has spiritual merit and one that is spiritually worthless or even downright harmful. This, of course, is precisely what the mystic has been saying all along: spiritual "knowing" has nothing to do with the mind, with logic, but rather is a matter of the "heart," that is, of the emotions or intuition.

The Bible, however, knows nothing of this kind of "knowing." When it speaks of knowing information, rather than persons, it means precisely that objective grasping of truth by the mind, according to normal, accepted definitions of that activity. This kind of knowledge is never shunned as unimportant or unspiritual. It is recognized as the absolutely necessary foundation for faith.

Evangelicals have long been prone to draw these kinds of mystical distinctions—distinctions where the "head," or mind, with its logical functions operating on concepts, is set in opposition to the "heart." In such a contrast, whether clearly stated or not, the mental functions are suspect, whereas the "heart" is seen as the spiritual "organ." This entire psychological notion is contrary to what the Scriptures actually teach.

What we fail to recognize is that implied in the foregoing contrast is a psychological theory that divides nonphysical man into at least two parts: the mind and the "heart." Most laymen and, I suspect, most ministers as well never stop to ask if this psychological theory has its basis in the Bible. Perhaps we thoughtlessly impose it on Scripture. If this theory is not actually stated by the Word, then we distort the Bible's meaning by our theory. This, unfortunately, seems to be what has happened.

The term *heart*, used in contrast to man's rationality, seems to have two possible meanings, although the one using the term may not be aware of such a dichotomy. It is used either as a synonym for inner, subjective urges and states, or else it indicates some special "organ" or faculty whose proper function is in the realm of the spiritual. Either of these two uses sets the heart at odds with the mind.[1]

If the first meaning is intended, the emotions are seen as a tool for knowing in the spiritual realm just as the mind is the proper tool for knowing in the physical world. In the second use, the heart is not identified with

1. This practice of distinguishing between mind and heart is a common one. For one recent example, which also has other features relevant to our topic, see the article entitled "Under Fire" in the Sept. 18, 1987, issue of *Christianity Today* magazine. The article reports a discussion between four men concerning certain mystical teachings and practices in which several of them are involved. In the discussion, heart seems to be variously equated with intuition and emotion and is clearly set in opposition to the mind. This allows certain statements and views to go unchallenged that should not be, and makes it appear that to follow intuition is biblical, when it is not.

the emotions. It is, however, still a nonmental, nonlogical function—not bound by the rules of logic. Nevertheless, it duplicates the activity of the mind, at least to the extent that one of its activities is to "know." Thus, the person is seen to have a special, unique organ or faculty whose purpose is to do for him in the spiritual realm what the mind does in the physical. Does the Bible teach either of these two closely related positions? The clear answer is that it does not.

REBUTTAL OF MYSTICISM'S INFILTRATION

A careful examination of the New Testament terms translated *heart*, and the Old Testament parallel term that the King James Version translates *reins*, will show that they have a number of related meanings. These may all be grouped under four classifications: (1) the will: it is with the heart that man decides and thus becomes obedient to the gospel (Rom. 6:17); (2) the emotions: it is with the heart that man feels grief and sorrow (Rom. 9:2); (3) the mind: with the heart man thinks and reasons (Mark 2:6);[2] and (4) the entire person—that is, the totality of man, make up of the mind, the will, and the emotions working together in the way God created them to do. It is the entire person, affected and distorted by sin, that is evil and in need of regeneration (Jer. 17:9).[3]

By observing these variations in meaning of *heart* in the Bible, it seems clear that consistently to contrast the concepts of *heart* and *mind* does violence to the Word.

It should be noted that those who separate mind and heart seem to have forgotten what Jeremiah tells us: "The heart is more deceitful than all else and is desperately

---

2. Gordon H. Clark, in his book *Faith and Saving Faith* (Jefferson, Md.: Trinity Foundation, 1983), p. 66, says that heart ". . . at least seventy-five percent of the time in the Old Testament means mind or intellect."
3. It should be noted that these references are merely representative. The reader can, and should, verify what I have said by using an unabridged concordance as he studies the Word to see whether or not this is correct.

sick; who can understand it?" (Jer. 17:9). If the heart is somehow a special spiritual organ by which we know spiritual things and the mind is not involved, why does Jeremiah see it as a predictable source of deceitfulness? One might argue, of course, that it is deceitful only in its unregenerated state, and that after God has cleansed it, it is no longer deceitful. But if this view is accepted, we must keep two things in mind. First, the verse does not clearly say that this refers to the unregenerate. Second, if God can so correct the "heart," why is He not equally willing to keep the mind of the regenerated person from error? And if He is, why make the heart a special organ for knowing? It seems obvious both from Scripture and from everyday experience that God created man to know and understand with the mind.

Those passages that refer to knowing with the heart must be understood in one of two ways if we are to be true to the entire teaching of the Bible. Either the texts simply refer to the mind, or else they refer to cognitive knowledge, including the proper active effect on the entire person. In some texts, both meanings may be legitimate possibilities. The context of each statement usually determines which of these is the correct meaning.

God created us as unified entities, integrated personalities in which the components are dynamically interrelated. Thus, when the mind grasps a fact, the emotions are appropriately affected. The effect on the emotions is generally appropriate to the information received by the mind. If the mind recognizes danger, fear will be the emotion. If it recognizes benefit, pleasure will be felt. The intensity of emotion may vary somewhat from person to person. Nevertheless, the specific emotions felt will generally be the same as long as both people understand the same information, and both are emotionally healthy.

It is important to notice that this mental-emotional interelationship is God-created and it functions automatically in a normal person. The key to emotional experience is mental understanding.

One of the proper functions of emotion is to prompt us to action. However, before proper action can be taken we must understand the situation. This involves recognizing some information about the problem, believing that information, and recognizing what action is appropriate. If, for the sake of clarification and convenience we treat the human being as consisting of mind, will, and emotion, then the understanding is the proper function of the mind, and the decision to act that of the will. Emotions can properly do their work only after the mind and the will have done theirs.[4]

If, then, we try to impose a different activity on any one of these factors in man, we distort God's created order. This is what happens when we somehow try to make the emotions do the job God has assigned to the mind. The truth of a claim must be settled by the use of rational means, not by considering how we "feel about it." Once the question of truth is decided, then the emotions should impel us to carry through on an appropriate response.

By drawing the usual distinction between "head" and "heart," evangelicals not only distort the meaning of the Scripture, but they also endanger the proper place of the written Word of God. If there is a "heart knowledge" that is of a different kind from a rational grasp of the propositions of Scripture, and if this is the superior kind of "knowledge," then the Bible, and our knowledge of it, is reduced to a place of secondary importance. We must keep in mind that what makes evangelical Christianity truly evangelical is the place it gives to the Bible as *the* source of all knowledge concerning salvation. From

4. This, admittedly, is a very superficial and poor description of a highly complex series of interrelated activities. Man is a much more complicated and marvelous creation than this description indicates. However, for our purposes, this simple analysis may serve to help us understand something of the distortion that concerns us here.

God's creation man can know something about His existence, His holiness, and about His righteous demands.
This is evident to all men (Rom. 1:19-20). However, this
source does not provide what must be understood and
believed for salvation. We can know that only through
the special revelation of the Bible.

SUMMARY AND CONCLUSION

Once again we are back to the same place. A written
Scripture demands cognitive knowledge before its revelation can be effective in our lives. Of course, God expects
more than mere understanding. What we understand must
be believed—and acted upon. No one who understands
Christian theology would ever claim that mere understanding is sufficient. But then, claiming to have knowledge implies that he who understands the truth also as-
sents to it, that is, believes it to be true. But those who
draw the distinction between "head" and "heart" knowledge would insist that such understanding and assenting
is mere "head knowledge." What, then, is different about
"heart knowledge"?

By way of review, some who use these terms may
merely mean that knowledge must be acted upon to be
significant. "Head knowledge" is viewed as nothing
more than intellectual understanding, whereas "heart
knowledge" is truth understood, believed, and acted
upon. Those who mean this have a correct grasp of what
should be. However, they use language in a dubious way,
which opens the door to a mystical theory. This "heart
knowledge," then, is not another kind of knowledge at
all.

If, however, someone insists on a true difference,
claiming that "heart knowledge" is actually not cognitive, not subject to the laws of logic, then he is insisting
on a mystical "knowing." This is something of which the
Bible says nothing.

3

THE ALLURE OF MYSTICISM:
Heart Cry for Spirituality

Mystical experience is influencing society through contemporary religious movements in various ways. I can only mention certain key issues. Therefore the following are just generalizations concerning selected aspects of the theme.

SOME VARIATIONS OF SPIRITUAL EXPERIENCES

To those who have had some contact with mystical movements, oriental religions are prime examples. The popularity in the West of movements such as Transcendental Meditation, the Divine Light Mission, and Hare Krishna, which are all varieties of Hinduism, is due to the appeal of mysticism. Interest in these movements was sparked during the late 1960s, largely through drug use and the popularity of rock music. Hinduism grew out of the ancient Vedic religions of India, which in turn seemed to have been influenced by drug experiences.

As we have already seen, religious drug use is an attempt to induce mystical experience. Serious mystics often maintain either that drugs are only a way of starting the process or that a drug experience is a counterfeit mys-

tical experience, not to be confused with "the real thing."
The appeal of rock music results, at least to some degree,
from its power to "alter consciousness," that is, to induce
a low-grade hypnotic state. This altered state, although
usually vastly less intense than a mystical experience,
seems to be closely related to it. Some people consider
the terms *mystical* and *occult* to be synonymous. Although this is inaccurate, many occult practices also involve mystical experiences.[1] Thus, the drug culture, oriental religion of all kinds, occultism, many of the new
non-Christian movements, and certain aspects of contemporary Christianity all have mystical experience as a
common element. This fact should make Christians cautious.

The attraction of many recent religious movements
depends on the claim that some living prophet has had
direct contact with God through a "personal experience."
This contact has resulted in a new revelation. The leader
has the key to power. This power is said to be available
for many purposes, especially for peace of mind, material
prosperity, or physical healing. Sometimes occult powers, such as clairvoyance, are promised. Investigation reveals that the promised power is usually related to
mystical experience. "Revelations" come by such experiences, and the promised results are said to come either
from learning to self-induce such experiences (usually
through meditation techniques) or from group sessions
that attempt to induce mystical trance states.[2]

1. See A. L. Langguth, *Macumba* (New York: Harper & Row, 1975), for a description of occult practices in Brazil. In Langguth's account the line between possession and mystical trance states can be seen as almost
non-existent.
2. For an example of one such group session, see Jack Sparks, *The Mind
Benders* (Nashville: Thomas Nelson, 1977), pp. 219-21. Although in this
case no intent to induce a mystical experience is meant, all indications
point to such an attempt. However, this would certainly be a low-grade experience and not one of deep intensity.

In other movements the "prophet" is said to have discovered the secret of "the power of God," "the mind," or of some aspect of the universe. Again, the "secret" was revealed through a mystical experience. This prophet asks believers to adopt a mystical attitude. This attitude is often described as "having faith."

As Christians, our tendency is to concern ourselves with the doctrines of those religions we believe to be wrong. This is a proper response and must not be neglected. When we are contending for the truth with one who accepts the Scriptures and applies legitimate hermeneutics to the task of understanding the Word, we have a common ground from which to work. Of vital importance is that the Bible is a public, objective criterion with a fixed, single meaning for everyone. However, in the case of mystically based systems, there is no objective criterion, no common ground from which to work.

The difficulty that so many Christians face results from the fact that, although they may not themselves be mystics, they have allowed their thinking to become confused by mystically inspired explanations of doctrinal positions. As a result, they are afraid to take a stand against mysticism within Christianity, lest they be found fighting against God. This fear stems from ignorance—ignorance of the Word, of mysticism, and of the nature of God Himself.

To help us see more clearly the influence of mystical views on evangelical Christianity and the danger that results from it, and to stimulate our thinking, I wish to make some preliminary remarks. These will be developed and argued in greater depth in later chapters.

First, just what do we mean when we speak of "being spiritual"? Careful study of the text of Scripture can reveal the biblical writers' intended meaning. It means to be under the control of the Holy Spirit to such an extent that maturity and holy living are produced. Not only is that life one of moral purity, but it also exhibits the fruit of the Spirit (Eph. 5:9, Gal. 5:22-23). This, however, is not what most people understand by the term. The world uses this phrase to mean something closely akin to "being mystical." For most people a heavy element of the emotional and the subjective permeates the meaning of *spiritual*.

Tragically, many Christians have adopted the world's use. As already mentioned, the problem of guidance plays a part here. This is only one result of a confusion that is traceable to the influence of the German idealists and later to the existentialists, as well as to the theological liberals of the early part of this century. All these taught, in one form or another, that religion is a matter of the feelings, not first of the mind, and that faith is an emotional state.[3] God's Spirit is believed to be an influence or an urge, and the point of contact between the individual and this impersonal force is through the emotions. This, however, is incorrect. To be spiritual is a relationship between the human person and the infinite Person, God. It is identical with being a maturing Christian. It is not primarily a psychological category. It has as great rational (conceptual) and volitional dimensions as emotional. Perhaps for clarity, we should give up using the phrase "being spiritual" and speak instead of "being godly."

The confusion that makes mysticism a present danger for Christianity may be more clearly seen if we examine the misunderstanding that exists in three areas: the nature of spiritual experience, the place of reason in the Christian life, and the nature of God's promised guidance of the believer. The first of these three areas will be our concern in the remainder of this chapter.

3. It should be noticed that I am not denying that our emotions have a place, but rather that the process begins logically with the mind. From there, the entire man is to be affected, not the emotions only or even primarily.

In the lives of many Christians there are those special times that we remember as highlights. Occasionally one of these events becomes a turning point. Before this time our Christianity lacked the intensity, the vitality, the reality that it seemed to assume thereafter. Quite often such an experience is charged with deep emotion. Often there is a series of emotions, such as deep conviction of sinfulness, followed by great sorrow and confession, and, finally, a sense of deep peace. At other times the feelings may be described as intense joy or acceptance by God. These events, as well as others like them, are what people generally mean when they speak of "spiritual experiences."

Having such experiences is both good and proper. However, they may also be the source of grave problems because of a misunderstanding of the Bible's teaching on these occurrences and misperception of their nature, source, and importance. It will be necessary, therefore, to examine spiritual experiences in some detail.

Some Definitions of Spiritual Experiences

The confusion in which many find themselves seems to stem from at least two sources: the first and most important is a lack of clear understanding of the word *spiritual*; the second concerns the nature and proper function of experiences.

It is important that we recognize that both these words, *spiritual* and *experience*, can be used in different ways. The word *spiritual* is especially troublesome because Christians often have confused two distinct meanings without recognizing that they have done so.

Too often we have adopted the world's idea of spirituality that sees it as a kind of psychological state with no reference to content. If a person is said to be a "spiritual person" we are to understand that he is "other worldly," not concerned with the everyday, mundane affairs of this world. Sometimes he is seen as a high-principled, intro-spective person, and usually one who pays serious atten-tion to his own subjective urges, impressions, and states. Thus, he is a person who has a basic tendency toward mys-ticism. Although Christians may not generally be aware of it, the world sees the committed mystic as the prime example of the "spiritual" person.

The world, of course, takes an ambiguous attitude to-ward such a person. In today's materialistic society such a person may be seen as totally impractical, unrealistic, and foolish. On the other hand, as a result of the growing public approval of mysticism, many people respect such a person as an ideal.

The Christian usually sees no such ambiguity toward "being spiritual." The biblical writers clearly contrast spirituality with worldliness. Most Christians, therefore, see being spiritual as the goal to be sought. But now we see the problem. Having uncritically (and perhaps un-consciously) accepted the world's definition of the term, it is only natural for them to look with favor on mysticism. This, however, is far from what the Scriptures teach as the believer's desirable goal.

Just what does it mean to be spiritual? Ask the aver-age member of an evangelical church; you may be sur-prised by the answers. My own experience indicates that one or another of several things may happen with only rarely positive results. The question may embarrass the one you ask; he may admit that he has never really thought about it. Then, you may get an answer that is ba-sically a set of vague phrases. These require careful defin-ition in their own right before they can be enlightening. Unless you pursue the issue further, it is impossible to tell whether or not he really understands at all. Finally, the response you are given may be some form of the mys-tical definition of the secular world. Only rarely have I found people whose meaning for the term fits the biblical use.

What, then, is biblical spirituality? To be spiritual is to be fully human in the sense that we are what God intended us to be.[4] At places in Scripture, "spiritual maturing" might be a synonym; at other places, "godliness" carries the same basic meaning.

God did not create us to be totally autonomous. We are not self-sufficient. We do not function well when we try to be. He made us to be totally reliant on Him. Thus, we are most nearly what He created us to be when the Holy Spirit is most completely in control. But to say this is not to say that we sit back and do nothing. In one's personal experience of the Holy Spirit's control, there will still be struggle and effort. Seen from human perspective, it will seem that what we do is accomplished by our own efforts. We will make decisions; we will carry out those decisions; we will feel the pain of what seems like failure; and we will enjoy the pleasure of success. This is because when the Spirit is in control He enables us to do what He wills. He uses our minds, our wills, and our emotions.

At the same time, we must remember that He created us as personal entities. We have minds with which to discover and grasp truth—minds that function according to the laws of logic when they operate correctly. When we understand and believe some bit of information, our God-given emotions respond somewhat appropriately. God also created us with the ability to decide to will, to act. To be under the control of the Holy Spirit, then, does not mean to be without self-control. Nor does it mean to act on impulse, as though He worked in us only through our

4. I am indebted for this definition to Ranold Macauley and Jerram Barrs, authors of *Being Human* (Downers Grove, Ill.: Inter-Varsity, 1978).

emotions. To be under His control is to act in accord with His direction as given in His Word, all parts of our being functioning as He created them to function. This means that we will seek all the necessary information, evaluating it according to the principles revealed in God's Word, with a deep desire to know the truth. Our decisions and judgments will be based on God's Word. Our emotions will respond to the truth, motivating us to carry out the wise decisions that our Spirit-controlled wills have made.

The result of all this will be a life that exhibits holiness in behavior, reverence for God, and respect for other people. It will be characterized by love, joy, peace, patience, kindness, goodness, faithfulness, gentleness, and self-control—all the fruit of the Holy Spirit.

But, unfortunately, there is another element that must be acknowledged—our sinfulness. We are fallen creatures. Therefore, we will not always be spiritual. There will be times when we do not fully yield to the Spirit's control. At times we will not acknowledge the truth. We will be self-willed; we will make foolish decisions. Tragically, we will rebel and violate what we know to be the truth. But God, in His great mercy, extends forgiveness.

Thus, biblical spirituality is as different from mysticism as it is possible to be. It is not merely a subjective experience of trust in one's inner, nonrational urges. Rather it involves the complete person functioning as God intended him to function.

We have seen something of the nature of biblical spirituality and the confusion that often exists about that concept. The word *experience* may also be a source of confusion since it too can be used ambiguously. At one extreme of a continuum of uses, anything of which I am vitally aware is part of my experience. Writing these words is an experience, as is the feel of the pen in my hand, the scratch of an uncomfortable shirt collar, the sound I hear from the piano in the next room, and the comforts of the fire in my fireplace. Experience, in these situations, means little more than "awareness." However, when one speaks of some spiritual experience it is unlikely that he is using the word in this sense.

The other extreme involves the intensity of the emotions experienced in a crisis. For example, when someone recounting an incident of great danger to himself, refers to the event as "quite an experience" he is using the word *experience* in this sense. Although the emotions may be simple or complex, it is the emotional intensity that is being stressed by this usage of *experience*.

These two uses of the term *experience* seem to be the extreme opposites. When people speak of "spiritual experience" they probably have in mind a meaning more like the second extreme than the first. What is highlighted is the intensity of the event, an intensity that can be sustained for only a relatively brief period of time. Consequently, such an event can be identified as having happened within a brief time period. It is this feature that makes it possible for some people to tell years later the exact date and hour when they had some significant experience.

We can now develop a popularized, working definition of the term *spiritual experience*. It is an event of fairly brief duration, having a rather intense emotional dimension, which the involved person believes to have spiritual significance. We should notice that this definition tells us nothing about what the person means by *spiritual*, whether such an experience is good or bad, or whether it is somehow from God or not. People of all religions have "spiritual experiences," as do some atheists. Therefore we are totally unjustified in assuming that such experiences are necessarily good or appropriate.

SOME RESTRICTIONS OF SPIRITUAL EXPERIENCES

It is at this point that some Christians encounter dangers. They either are not aware that the possibility exists of being deceived or else they cannot test their experiences. As a consequence, they are led astray. But before we explore exactly what happens, it will be useful to examine the positive aspects of spiritual experiences.

God has created us to function in some very definite ways, though this created order is affected by sin and often operates in a distorted way. In the matters we are considering, we are made to respond in very appropriate ways to information. When someone fails to respond in certain ways we recognize that something has gone wrong. If, for example, we are told that the house is on fire, we will feel fear and will leave the building. If, however, someone does not leave but continues as before with no evidence of fear, we will assume that either he did not believe what was told him, or he is insane. On the other hand, if someone constantly feels fear without any identifiable basis for it we will say that he also has psychological problems. In short, the normal person exhibits a certain appropriate kind of relationship between what he believes to be true and what he feels.

When we are functioning properly our emotions vary according to our beliefs in several ways. They vary with the content of belief, the depth of our understanding, and the degree of our belief. Danger elicits fear, beauty causes pleasure. An unusual sight may produce wonder, but greater understanding of what is being observed may vastly increase or decrease the degree of wonder. If I am fully convinced of the truth of something my emotions will be more intense than if I am still uncertain.

We must keep in mind that the intensity of emotion will vary from person to person. We are each unique, having our own personal histories, and this affects our emotional responses. We should recognize, too, that our personal responses will vary from time to time because they are also linked to our physical states. If I am ill, my responses to a truth may be vastly different in intensity from what they would be if I were in good health. Consequently, I dare not use the degree of emotional intensity that is part of some experience as a significant indicator of my spiritual state and the Holy Spirit's working in me.

It is tragic that many people see the intensity of their emotional responses as the one significant indicator of their faith. When this happens, the problem may be quite complex, involving a false concept of faith itself. Even when our view of the nature of faith is reasonably correct, we create problems for ourselves when we use our emotions as indicators of the degree of our trust in God. We often develop guilt feelings when the intensity of our emotions cools. How many sermons have you heard about losing one's "first love," where love is measured, not by behavior, or even loyalty, but by one's emotional intensity? We may think we have failed in our faith simply because our emotions are low. On the other hand, we might wrongly think that our relationship to God is correct simply because our emotions are high. Both attitudes are unjustified.

Problems raised by giving an improper place to subjective experience tend to complicate every major aspect of the Christian life and of our relationship to God. The perversion of faith is one significant example of this. Christians acknowledge the central place of faith. Without faith it is impossible to please God. We are saved by faith. The just shall live by faith. All these are basic concepts without which true Christianity cannot exist. Yet it is amazing how few Christians clearly understand the biblical concept of faith; and it is one of the great tragedies of our day that so many confuse faith with subjective feelings and thereby, in the name of faith, refuse to practice faith.

Faith must not be equated with emotional experience. Although our faith will affect our emotions, we create serious problems when we identify faith and feeling as intrinsically the same. Our faith in God is to be based on God, not on us and how we feel. To equate faith and feeling results in trusting in ourselves and not in God.

What has just been said constitutes very serious charges that ought not to be made lightly. They can be accepted only if adequately explained and verified. It will, therefore, be good to turn our attention first of all to the nature of faith and later to the defense of the charge that in the name of faith many refuse to practice true faith. What, then, is faith? It is tempting to say that it is simply belief or trust. But biblical faith is more, much more, than what most people understand by either belief or trust. The "much more," however, is not an emotional element, as is often implied. Rather it is the interrelationship of belief and trust, and a full understanding of this involves faith's foundation and its result.

To begin, we must understand what it means to believe something. To say, "I believe," is to say that I acknowledge the truth of something. The first element in faith, then, is truth. But what does it mean to say that some statement is true? It means that that statement gives us an accurate representation of the part of reality of which it speaks. To believe something is to acknowledge that statement as providing an accurate picture of reality.

At this point, all we have is an intellectual, passive concept. This is not faith, although it is an absolutely essential aspect of faith. Without belief, "faith" is not faith. For belief to be genuine belief it also must have content. We cannot believe without having something to believe. Now, this is different from feeling because it is possible to feel most individual emotions without having a sound basis for any one of them. For example, I can feel fear without having any good cause for being afraid. If this happens too often I am exhibiting a psychological abnormality. However, the point here is that this is not so about belief. I cannot experience believing without believing *something* to be true.

The second element in faith is trust. This is confidence in the object about which we now think we have the truth. If we are speaking of faith in God, the belief concerns statements about God, which we take to be true and which result in our trusting God. The statements relate to His nature and show us, first of all, that He is trustworthy. They also contain His promises. On the basis of His promises and His nature we come to trust Him. This trust leads to a settled life commitment, which the Bible calls "faith in God."

What, then, is trust or confidence? Is it not a feeling? It may have a feeling accompanying it—a "feeling of confidence." But confidence is simply a recognition of fact, or of correctness. Thus, confidence in the truthfulness of God's statements is the recognition, for instance, that He cannot lie.

We should notice the vital importance of truth in our faith. Faith might rest on error, but if it does it is worse than worthless. If I trust that the liquid in a bottle will relieve a headache when in reality it is a deadly poison, my faith will have disastrous consequences. The value of faith depends absolutely on the correctness of what we believe.

An important assumption in this discussion is that we understand the biblical statements we are asked to believe. We cannot believe statements whose sense we do not grasp. Even if the statements are true but we misunderstand them, we will be believing something other than what the statements actually say. Correct understanding of the truth is absolutely necessary for a proper faith.

At this point, the voices of mysticism rise in protest. Their attention here is on the feeling, not on the reasonableness of trusting based on truth. Some even go so far as to assert that if rational processes, such as the process we have suggested earlier, are involved, then this is not faith. Faith, they say, stands in opposition to reason. Faith is an attitude that ignores, if not violates, what reason indicates to be true. Others insist that it is not yet faith if there is good reason to believe something to be true. It is faith only if it goes beyond what reason tells us is true.

Lest we misunderstand, we must pause here to clarify the issues. Part of the confusion results from an inadequate understanding of what is meant by the terms *reason* and *rationality*. By these terms are meant the God-given powers of thought and reasoning. To act rationally, then, means to act in accordance with what one understands and takes to be true. If I come to understand that God loves me, that He desires only my best, that He is all-wise, all-knowing, and almighty; and if I come to believe this to be true, then the rational response is to trust Him with my life. If, on the other hand, I come to believe that He hates me, or that He is capricious, or impotent, or unwilling to help me, then it is rational to refuse to trust Him.

Now, it seems that this is not what some people mean by being rational. Due to the influence of contemporary scientific attitudes, they see rationality demanding the presuppositions of inductive reasoning and sensory experience. From this they conclude that because God is not open to direct physical verification, no statement about Him should ever be said to be true. *True* and *false*, as well as *fact*, are usable terms only for statements that can be verified through science. Therefore, they say, no statements about God can meet the requirement we have set as the basis for faith, that is, a rational grasp of the truth and assent to that fact. If this is so, they reason, then faith must be that feeling of confidence people have about things not open to scientific verification.

Others argue as though the words *reason* and *rationality* imply certain other, usually naturalistic, presuppositions. Reason, they say, deals only with facts in the world and with questions about whether or not those facts are real things or events in the physical realm. Thus, they suggest, to speak of knowledge of God as being based on reason is a contradiction, for God (if He exists) is not part of the "natural" world. Because only the natural world is real, and nature is all there is, God can exist only in our thoughts. To reach such a God, we must look within ourselves. I confess that it is difficult to see how this makes any sense, for it sounds suspiciously like a contradiction. Nevertheless, some well-meaning people, influenced by naturalistic reasoning, reject any suggestion that faith should be rationally based. Again, their only alternative seems to be to say that faith refers only to something subjective, with no objective aspects.

There are at least two things wrong with seeing faith as only in emotional, rather than rational, terms. First, this is not the biblical picture. The Scripture does not place the emphasis on our feelings, but rather on the truth and our recognition of, and assent to, that truth. Thus, the attention is not on the amount of faith we have, but on God's faithfulness.

The second thing that is wrong with this scheme of things results from the changeable nature of our feelings. As my feelings vary my confidence will vary also, if it rests on my emotions. It is because God is unchangeable that my confidence in Him can remain constant. To equate faith with feeling is, in reality, a denial of the faithfulness of God.

Another subtle aspect of this outlook becomes apparent when someone seeks feelings as verification of his faith. Although he may not express it in so many words, he is really saying that God's Word is true only when he feels it is true. When he does not feel confident, then God's statements have become doubtful. In the name of what he calls faith, he is refusing to trust God.

But someone may ask, "If feelings are not the test of faith, then what is?" This is an important question. James answers this question (James 2:18). Not what I say, nor yet how I feel, but what I do, is the test of my faith. Having faith in God will mean that I will use my time wisely. Faith is shown by correct behavior. It is confident trust in his promises expressed in appropriate action. If I truly believe that God is totally righteous, and if I also believe that He has said that we are not to take His name in vain, my language will be different.

There are, no doubt, many things that contribute to a distorted view of faith, but I wish to mention only one more. The way we handle Scripture shows what we believe its nature and place to be. When we read Bible passages primarily as a means of giving ourselves an emotional lift, we tend to ignore the actual meaning of the passage. Whatever it "says to me," regardless of what was the actual intent of the writer, is taken as the Spirit's intent. My own emotional needs or desires dictate the meaning I read into the passage.

Although it may not be quite accurate to call this experience-oriented interpretation of Scripture mysticism, it shares with mysticism many fundamental characteristics, such as a knowledge-through-emotions approach. It also prepares the person to trust mystical experience. Worst of all, it substitutes another criterion of knowledge and truth in spiritual matters instead of the Bible, while hiding this fact by making the Scriptures a tool for expressing one's emotional criterion. Thus, by tolerating or encouraging this approach to the Bible, some Christian leaders create the setting for mysticism, and through it, for mystically-based cults.

SUMMARY AND CONCLUSION

The problem, then, for the Christian finally resolves itself into the question of the nature, function, completeness, and interpretation of God's revelation, the Word. Is the Bible itself the revelation of God to us today, or is it only a tool for His revelation? Is it an empty vessel, itself devoid of significant revelatory meaning, into which the Holy Spirit pours subjective, private meaning? If the Scriptures are themselves the revelation of God, then they have a significant meaning, objectified in human language. This meaning is the same for all men. It does not change from person to person.

If this is the case, then it is of the most vital importance that I first come to know that truth before I determine its significance for myself. I must, of course, not stop there. Application is also vital, as James points out. But I cannot afford to allow anything to shift my attention from the message that the Holy Spirit put into the words of the Bible.

If, on the other hand, I depend on some subjective, inner feeling or urge, and not on the actual conceptual content of the passage to give me "the Spirit's meaning," I am guilty of practicing a form of mysticism. By my practice, I have denied the need for the written Word.

It is this attitude toward Scripture, this trust in subjective experience, and this experience-based interpretation of the Bible that are the real difficulties with the charismatic movement, and not primarily its attitude toward spiritual gifts. That attitude, especially as expressed in the practice of speaking in tongues (*glossolalia*) and "prophecy," is the result of a weak attitude toward the

Word. The charismatics' inadequate concept of the nature, function, and interpretative rules of the Bible have often left them wide open to mysticism. Many of their teachings seem to result from low-grade mystical experience. We mistake the problem and underestimate the danger if we fail to see this lack of adequate rational and biblical foundation.

4

THE ANTIDOTE OF MYSTICISM:
Restoration of Reason

Many Christians find themselves sympathetic to mysticism for another reason beside experience-centeredness. They have confused rationality with rationalism. This confusion must be avoided if, on the one hand, we are to see clearly the place of the Scriptures and to escape the problems of mysticism, and, on the other, we are to avoid reducing God's Word to mere human speculation.

The Evangelical Confusion About Human Reason

During much of this century it has been popular in conservative churches to treat rationalism as a significant attack of Satan on the faith of believers. Without a doubt, much of what has been said in this regard is both correct and proper. Unfortunately, however, the untutored layman and the inadequately trained pastor have often moved beyond this legitimate concern to the extreme of anti-intellectualism. Then, in an attempt to fill the void left by the rejection of intellectual understanding, many have turned to mysticism. If we are to avoid doing the same thing, we must have some grasp of both the proper and the improper uses of reason.

It may be that some of the confusion has resulted from the similarity of the two terms, *rationality* and *rationalism*. Rationalism is the general name for a group of theories that have in common the idea that all knowledge depends ultimately upon some natural quality in the human mind. The mind comes equipped from birth with broad principles that make it possible for man to develop all knowledge without dependence on any outside source. A variant position claims that man needs sensory input to provide the raw material for knowledge, but he is not seen to need anything from any other mind, not even the mind of God. Thus, both the source of all knowledge and the final criterion of all truth is said to be human reason.

Rationality, on the other hand, refers to the ability to understand and think according to the rules of logic. Used in the general sense, it is the God-given ability that makes man distinct from animals, that ability which we all use in every aspect of our lives. For our purposes, the two words, rationality and reason, mean nearly the same thing.

It is not our purpose here to concern ourselves with theories of knowledge that are forms of rationalism and at the same time claim to be true to biblical Christianity. In general, I believe it is correct to say that most forms of rationalism proposed in the past have stood in opposition to Christianity. There are several reasons for this.

This is primarily so because biblical Christianity is based on the position that all knowledge of God begins with God's revelation. The ultimate source of truth is God Himself. Since this is so, the ultimate standard by which truth is judged is God's revelation. Therefore, if the result of human reasoning stands in opposition to God's revelation, the Bible, the results of such reasoning must be rejected. To say, as rationalistic theories do, that man's reasoning ability is, itself, the final criterion against which all things must be tested before they can be declared true is to make man and not God ultimate. This is a form of blasphemy, since it ascribes to mere man what is the prerogative of God alone.

Reason, or rationality, then, is God's good gift, whereas rationalism is a theory that says that man has in himself the ability to discover all truth without the aid of God. Rationalism, of course, rejects the need for revelation and makes God's Word subject to the test of human reason. As Christians, we must reject such a theory.

Furthermore, biblical Christianity says that the Scriptures are the ultimate standard of *all* truth. This position goes beyond merely claiming that God's Word, and not human reason, is the ultimate standard of truth in spiritual matters. This means that any claim in any area that itself contradicts Scripture, whether explicitly or implicitly, is false.

This strong position must be maintained by the Christian if he is to be true to what the Bible says about itself, as well as to what it says about God. If God is truly almighty, all-knowing, all-good, unable to lie, and if He has communicated to man in the form of the written Word, then what He has said simply cannot be false in any way. If it is totally and absolutely true, then it follows that anything that disagrees with it must be false. When, therefore, men's ideas disagree with Scripture they are false. The Bible, and not human theories or abilities, is the ultimate criterion of all truth. There is no area of human investigation in which human reason can state total autonomy apart from any prior claim of God.

This is the position that Christians must maintain, and it is to a large degree the belief that identifies one as an evangelical Christian. Unfortunately, some have mistakenly believed that this means that all reasoning is bad. It is as though to say that reason is not the ultimate criterion of truth is the same as saying that rationality always leads to what is false. But when a Christian denies that reason is the ultimate criterion of truth he is not rejecting the process of thought. God's communication to man cannot be grasped, understood, or acted upon without the use of our God-given reasoning ability. The question is really not concerning reason itself, but rather about the content of human reasoning. Perhaps it would be even better to speak of the starting point for the reasoning process.

The Divine Intention for Human Reason

Part of the difficulty people have at this point has its roots in an historical confusion. The sixteenth, seventeenth, and eighteenth centuries are often called "the Age of Reason." It was during this period of time that rationalism reached its most prominent position in Western Europe. One of the interesting things that a careful examination of the literature of this period will reveal, however, is that although everyone talked about "reason," few defined it. The way the word was used showed that there were almost as many meanings for the word as there were writers using it. There was, it seems, one common element, and an unfortunate one at that.

Most writers used the word *reason* to designate the process by which they arrived at their beliefs. What they did not recognize is that whatever process one uses, that process operates upon some prior basis that is not part of the process itself. Thus, if one's process is strict logical deduction, for example, there must be some premises treated as true and on which the process of deduction is to operate before one can proceed. For lack of a better designation I will refer to this "beginning material" as the assumptions one makes. The term *assumptions* is appropriate here because these beginning points are usually taken for granted.

What these rationalistic writers did not realize was that the same rational process used to the same degree of accuracy by several thinkers will give as widely differing results as the differing assumptions with which the thinkers begin. In other words, the end product is determined at least as much by one's assumptions as by one's process.

Unfortunately, Christians have not recognized this fact any more clearly than did writers in the so-called Age of Reason. When an author argued that belief in miracles, for example, is "contrary to reason," it seems that Christians often believed that this was true. But if by reason we mean only the careful and accurate use of our minds in accordance with the rules of logic, such a statement is not true at all. The claim makes some sense only if we add to the meaning of reason what we have no right to do, namely the assumptions of naturalism.[1] And this is precisely what still happens every time some statement is made to the effect that Christianity violates reason. Tragically, Christians themselves have come to believe these false statements that spring from anti-Christian assumptions and biases.

An example of the tension between biblical faith and rationalism is in the area of modern science. It is naturalistic assumptions at the heart of much of scientific discussion that create many problems for Christians. Bible believers are told that the Bible contradicts science. They are also told that what has been "scientifically proved" is thereby shown to be absolutely true. They fail to recognize that the scientific method can never provide results that are absolute (something that every knowledgeable

1. By naturalism I mean the philosphical theory that insists there is no God, at least not one who in any way affects affairs here on earth. Thus, every event can be totally explained by referring only to other natural and physical events. For a more thorough explanation of naturalism and its implications, see James Sire, *The Universe Next Door* (Downers Grove, Ill.: Inter-Varsity, 1976), pp. 58-75.

scientist understands very well). Nor do believers realize that the word *science* may be used in several different ways. When science contradicts the Bible it does so because science here includes the theories that are based, at least in part, on naturalism. It is not the raw data with which the scientist works, nor yet the process of formulating hypotheses and testing them that results in the contradiction. Instead, it is the assumptions that result in a rationalistic interpretation of the data. Many of the theories of modern science do contradict the Bible, but these must be recognized for what they are: interpretations that originate with anti-supernatural assumptions.

It is easy to see why some sincere Christians are inclined to reject reason and promote anti-intellectualism. They believe the biblical accounts of creation, the Flood, and miracles. They believe the biblical claims that God is active in our lives and is able to intervene supernaturally. Unfortunately, however, they also tend to believe that science is the most accurate expression of reason. Confidence in science conditions Christians to believe the false claims of the naturalists that belief in creation and miracles runs counter to the dictates of reason. Thus, they feel forced to make a choice between God's Word and reason. In that situation, Christians often choose God's Word and reject reason. However, such a choice is unnecessary. There is no contradiciton between the Bible and the use of reason as such, but there is a great chasm between the Bible and the theory of naturalism.

No method by itself, regardless of its field, can ever guarantee true results. This is true of the rules of logic, as well as of the scientific method. Much of the time we are interpreting and evaluating data on the basis of doubtful assumptions. The correctness of the final results depends, to a much greater extent than most realize, on the correctness of those presuppositions.

If I begin by assuming that there is no God, I will arrive at false conclusions even if I follow the rules of logic without any error. Only by beginning with God and His truth can careful reasoning lead us to truth. It is imperative, therefore, that the thinking Christian bring his mind to the service of Christ while also examining his presuppositions in the light of the Word.

Christians, then, have no good grounds for rejecting reason. Furthermore, Christians cannot grasp God's truth without the use of this divinely given ability. The fact that God, in His sovereignty, chose to express His truth to us in rational words and ideas demonstrates that He intends for us to use our reasoning ability.

"But," someone may ask, "could God not communicate to us by some method that does not use our reason? Is He not free to do what He pleases? And since He is, may He not relate to us through some form of mysticism?"

This is certainly a fair question, but it shows a basic misunderstanding. It is true that God is not "boxed in" by some method imposed on Him from the outside. He is free to choose whatever procedure He wishes. However, He is not free to violate His own rational nature. This is so, not because of something outside Himself, but because of His very essence. He is unchanging and unchangeable (Heb. 1:12; 13:8), and He cannot lie (Titus 1:2). The question is not what God is capable of doing, but rather what He has chosen to do. God has not shown either by example or by direct statement that mystical experience is a method He has chosen by which to accomplish His purposes.

For someone, then, to argue that God does speak to us through mystical means merely on the basis of the general fact that He is able to do so, is a violation of available evidence that such teaching transgresses the prohibition against saying in God's name what He has not said (Deut. 18:20).

THE EMOTIONAL BY-PRODUCT OF HUMAN REASON

The Christian, then, is bound by God's sovereign choice to the use of his reasoning ability as he relates to God. This will shock and dismay some very sincere Christians for several reasons. It will seem to depersonalize God and make their relation to Him a cold, sterile thing. This also will seem to strip their faith of emotion and thus reduce Christianity to little more than rational assent. None of this is really true.

Let's recall certain facts. Faith in God depends on the truth of God's statements.[2] We have been created in such a way that if we are emotionally healthy people we will experience emotions that are appropriate to what we believe. Appropriate emotions will vary in degree as our understanding and certainty of the issues fluctuate.

We must not forget, however, that we are fallen creatures living in a fallen world. Our emotional response will never be perfectly what it should be. Perhaps even more significantly, it will never be what it should be because our understanding of God's truth will never be all it should be until we ultimately stand in God's presence in our redeemed bodies (Rom. 7:24-25).

But emotion there will be. If there is no feeling of joy, no sense of peace, no shame or sorrow for sin, no thankfulness for God's great salvation, no wonder at God's love, no humility and awe at the recognition of who God is, then it is doubtful that we understand God's truths. Without some degree of understanding there can be no faith; without faith there is no salvation. It may well be that he who never has any emotion is not a Christian. If this is so, however, it is not that his salvation somehow depends on his having certain emotions, but rather that both emotion and salvation depend on understanding and belief. (On the other hand, a lack of emotion may not

2. See the discussion of faith in chapter 3.

indicate a lack of faith at all, but rather an emotionally abnormal person. This type of person is not, however, the issue at this point.)

SUMMARY AND CONCLUSION

By now it should be clear that emotion is not a part of faith, but that the person who understands correctly will have emotions. But this is not to make our relationship to God an emotion. Perhaps an example will help.

When the relationship between husband and wife is what God intended, two normal people will feel an entire range of emotions. But it would be improper to say that their relationship *is* an emotion or even that it *depends on* emotions. The relationship depends on what they know to be true: their God-ordained mutual responsibilities and privileges, their commitment to God and to each other, and their love for each other. That love is a decision, constantly renewed, to seek each other's best. But what joy, what intense emotions, result from such a relationship. Just so it is with our relationship to God.[3] Emotions have their proper place as a result of our relationship, but that relationship does not depend solely on those emotions. Nor are emotions the proper way of knowing one has this relationship.

This, then, is the progression of the individual human-divine encounter. God extends His gracious revelation to man through the Bible and general revelation. Man receives the message of God from outside himself, and he thinks it over. Hopefully, man then responds appropriately to the message of God. If man trusts the Word of God, he will in due time experience the emotions of a heart in proper fellowship with its Savior and Lord.

---

3. See those parts of chapters 2 and 3 that deal with the relation that exists between belief and emotion.

5

THE RECURRENCE OF MYSTICISM:
Search for Guidance

One of the great advantages the Christian has over others is that God promises He will guide him in this life. His realization of this fact gives him great confidence and peace as he struggles with the problems of life that are common to all human beings.

Therefore, someone may question if it is appropriate to suggest that there are problems related to God's guidance of His children. But the truth is that many Christians find themselves facing significant problems in this area. At least some of the difficulty we experience results from faulty teaching on the subject. Often we have been taught that God leads us through a mystical "inner voice." For many, this poses no problem. However, what of those occasions when we follow what we believe to be the voice of God, and things turn out badly? Are we to say that God misled us? Or do we say that somehow the problem lay with us?

TRADITIONAL TEACHING ON DIVINE GUIDANCE

I have already suggested that many evangelical Christians are drawn into a form of mysticism because they have been taught that God leads by means of an inner, subjective experience. If this is not specifically a form of mysticism, it is so similar to mysticism that it is difficult to distinguish between the two. Once we have accepted this as God's means of guiding us, it becomes difficult for most of us to reject the idea that God may speak in this same way about many matters, even including doctrinal issues. Thus, accepting this theory of guidance opens the door for the acceptance of mysticism in other areas of one's life. We incur the problem of a faulty view of how God guides us and the danger of being led deeper into mysticism.

The position about divine guidance that has become traditional in evangelical circles involves an assumption that cannot be supported from Scripture, namely, that in no sense should *we* make our own decisions.[1] Rather, the "spiritual" thing to do is to leave all decisions to God. Thus, we must discover what God in His wisdom has determined for us.

Now, it should be emphasized that there are indeed areas in which we are not free to decide. I am not charged with the responsibility of deciding whether or not I should lie, cheat, steal, or murder. These actions are forbidden to me. Nor am I free to decide to marry an unbeliever, or to divorce my wife after I am married. These are also forbidden to me. On the other hand, I am not free to withhold love from others. I am commanded to love. But what about such questions as whether or not to buy an automobile, to go to the mountains for a vacation instead of to the seacoast, or to become a medical doctor

1. For an excellent discussion of this entire problem, see Garry Friesen, *Decision Making and the Will of God* (Portland, Oreg.: Multnomah, 1980). Friesen gives both the most complete and the most fair presentation of the traditional view I have seen. He also shows a position that he calls "the way of wisdom," which I agree is more biblical than the traditional view. The book is a significant contribution to the discussion of this entire subject.

rather than a lawyer? Here the Bible has nothing to say. Am I responsible to make these decisions?

If we answer the preceding question by saying we must discover God's specific plan for us in those matters, the next question is, "How are we to go about doing that?" We cannot appeal to the Bible for the direct answer, because it does not address my private life. Nowhere in it can I find any reference to whether or not I am to purchase an automobile this year or next year. I can find general principles about making wise decisions, even about wise monetary transactions, but no directives about exactly what God, in His wisdom, has determined for me in any specific situation. If He has decided these things for me, how am I to discover His will?

The answer that has become almost standard in evangelical circles usually involves three things. We are taught that we must take into account what the Bible says, the circumstances involved, and certain inner feelings. The latter are often described as "having peace." If the Bible does not forbid a course of action, and if circumstances make it possible or desirable, then the deciding factor becomes our inner urges. Sometimes, however, we are taught by plain statements or by the testimonies of others that God's decision may go contrary to all our circumstances. In these cases, the only one of the traditional guiding principles that remains is our inner impressions. How we are to determine whether or not today's decision should take circumstances into account is not usually made clear.

If we closely examine this traditional approach to divine guidance, we discover some interesting things. The appeal to Scriptures, as highly important as it is, will not really help here. The Bible does not give us God's specific directions for our individual decisions. Although it gives us significant principles that are useful and necessary if we are to make wise decisions, it does not tell us the details of our daily lives. Circumstances are also important factors if we are to make wise decisions, but how can they tell us God's plan for us?

There are always those who espouse an idea but never really practice it. It is this way in regard to divine guidance. Doubtless many who pay lip service to this traditional process really make their own decisions just as others do. They make their own decisions and do not somehow find God's decisions for their personal lives. Others, sincerely convinced of the correctness of the traditonal approach, struggle to find God's unique decision for their life choices. However, very few try to follow this scheme in the little decisions: which shoe to put on first in the morning, whether to eat an orange for breakfast or have juice instead.

BIBLICAL PRIORITY FOR DIVINE GUIDANCE

The traditional way of securing decisions forces me into a form of mysticism. I find myself appealing to my inner impressions that I identify as the voice of God. Because considering biblical principles and surrounding circumstances provides data that can help only if I make the decision, I can turn only to my inner impressions to find God's plan, if indeed I believe God alone can make my decisions. But this will not be sufficient if I see those impressions for what they really are, merely my inner states. If they were really the voice of Almighty God, only then could they serve in the capacity in which I need help.

At this point someone may be inclined to ask, "But cannot God guide in this way? After all, I have often had just such experiences, and I believe the decisons I made were God's will. Does this not prove that God leads in this way?" Aside from begging the question, these thoughts raise an important issue that must be clearly understood if we are to deal successfully with mysticism. It is the issue of the priority of Scripture.

In this connection, there are several principles of which we tend to lose sight. First, and of major importance, is that Scripture, and not our experience, is to be our final criterion of truth. This cannot be overemphasized. If the Scriptures do not clearly teach that this is God's designated way, then, even if we have made many crucial decisions on the basis of some inner voice, and made them with good results, this alone does not prove that we were led by the Spirit of God, nor that this is God's designated means for guiding us. To claim that it does is to say that experience, not Scripture, is our source and final test of all truth in these matters.

There is a corollary to this principle of Scripture priority to which we must also be sensitive. God, we know, is able to do anything and is free to do whatever He chooses. The question that concerns us here, then, is not what He is able to do, but rather what method He has chosen to use in guiding us. This we can discover only from God's revelation, the Bible.

This issue may become clearer if we look at a biblical case and examine some of its implications. God, in His mercy, once gave guidance to a man through a donkey. He gave the donkey the ability to speak and thereby affected the behavior of the man (Num. 22:20-30).[2] Yet no one who really understands what the Bible teaches about God's communication with men would expect Him to use this means to guide someone today. God is certainly able to do so, and He has demonstrated that very ability. Although God is both free and able to use many and varied means to guide us, our concern should be to determine His revealed means. Even though God, in His great mercy, may use other means, we are being presumptuous

---

2. It is, I think, significant to notice that in this incident it is not the donkey who delivers God's message. This is done by the angel of the Lord.

when we put our trust in things that God has not designated as His means. The question, then, becomes, Is an inner, subjective "voice" one of God's specified methods for leading us today? The answer to that question must be found in a careful study of Scripture.[3]

Although it is not within the scope of this book actually to do such a study, I believe a careful examination of Scripture will not support any mystical method as the means by which God guides us. Those passages that have been widely used to support the teaching that God uses inner peace, or some similar subjective impression, as a factor in His guidance, on careful scrutiny will be found to refer to other matters.[4]

The Bible teaches that the Holy Spirit will lead us, but we are never told that He will do this by some inner urge. It is interesting in this connection that when Jesus told His disciples that He would send the Holy Spirit and that the Spirit would lead them into all truth, He said, "He will teach you all things, and bring to your remembrance all that I said to you" (John 14:26). Here the leading is by bringing to mind Jesus' statements. The mind of each disciple is the instrument the Spirit will use, not some nonrational, mystical factor.

3. As noted earlier (chapter 1, note 4), there are no clear cases of mystical experience mentioned in Scripture. There are, however, two alleged cases: that which is referred to by Paul (2 Cor. 12:1-4) and King Saul's experience with the sons of the prophets (1 Sam. 19:20-24). Although we are given too little information to conclusively decide whether or not these cases were indeed mystical, it is most significant that, even though these might have been mystical events, the Holy Spirit does not record any information, doctrine, or guidance that resulted from them. Nor do any didactic passages in Scripture promote mystical experience as a means of God's leading. What is clearly taught, however, is the wise, careful use of the mind in making decisions. For a few examples see the following passages from the Proverbs: 11:14, 15:14 and 22, 19:20, and 24:5-6.
4. Friesen, *Decision Making*, pp. 137-44. Friesen examines three passages that are often used as the basis for the claim that God uses inner peace as an indicator of His leading: Col. 3:15, Phil. 4:7, and Gal. 5:22. He shows that none of these teach what they are often said to teach, as a careful examination of their contexts will show.

IMPORTANT QUESTIONS ABOUT DIVINE GUIDANCE

If what I have said is true, then we are faced with something of a puzzle. It is usually the safest course of action to be cautious when we are asked to abandon beliefs that have been widely accepted for some time. Yet I am claiming that the traditional view of divine guidance is wrong and should be discarded. Some questions that will arise in the mind of readers, and which demand answers, are these: If the traditional view is wrong, how did it develop? Why has it not been seriously challenged long ago?

I have already suggested some answers. The development of the traditional view was partly due, I believe, to the confusion about the nature of spirituality, which we discussed in chapter 3. No doubt there were other forces that contributed to it also, but I suspect the confusion played a major part. This, as well as all the other aspects of the mysticism we find among evangelicals, also goes a long way toward explaining why this view has not been challenged long before now. To do so would have been viewed as something distinctly unspiritual. After all, it sounds so right to say that we do not make our own decisions, but we seek God's decisions for us.

There is, I believe, another aspect we must take into account, one that indicates a motivational problem. Many people find it hard to make decisions and then accept the responsibility for the results of them. It would be so nice if someone else told us what to do when we had those key choices to make. Part of the problem is that we rarely have all the information we need to avoid making occasional mistakes. As a result, making the decision is always risky, especially when much depends on what we do.

At this point the Christian may see himself in the unique situation of having Someone available who knows all things, and beside, One who controls the very universe. Why not turn to Him for help? And, of course, this is correct. We have the greatest privilege in the entire universe. We can ask counsel of the Source of all wisdom and power. This is not, however, where the problem lies.

We face problems when we fail to see that God has so ordered things that He intends for us to make those decisions in our lives where the choices involved do not violate His moral will. Why He has so ordained things we are not told. Without question, He is capable of telling us just what to do in every detail of our lives, but He has not chosen to do so. Instead, we reap the positive results for wise decisions and suffer the consequences for foolish ones. Some people, however, seem to try to avoid their responsibilities by believing they can hear God giving them detailed instructions. The motivation behind the traditional view, at least in part, may be the wish to avoid the frightening responsibility involved in decision-making.

Does this mean that God does *not* lead us in the details of our lives? Certainly not. What it does mean is that He leads us as we make our own decisions. True wisdom is of Him. His guidance is by means of the Holy Spirit's influence on our minds as we seek to gather the pertinent facts and understand and apply the biblical principles to the situation at hand (John 16:12-14; Rom. 12:2). It means that He directs our wills as we struggle with the decision. He is involved in every aspect of the process to the extent that we allow Him to be.

What it does *not* mean is that we will have some special emotional or intuitive experience that gives us God's unique decision in the matter. We will not be aware of having some experience significantly different from that which all people have as they struggle to make wise decisions. The difference between the Christian's decision-making process and that of the non-Christian lies not in some subjective experience, but rather in the fact that

God has promised to give us wisdom. We can rest on that promise and move with confidence, not in our own wisdom, but in His.

But even when we correctly apply biblical principles God has not promised that we will necessarily see the truth immediately, nor has He promised that the process will be without struggle.

We must keep in mind that God is in the process of developing us into the "image of His Son" (Rom. 8:28-29). He may use even our foolish decisions to further that purpose. The process of learning to make wise decisions is a process that takes time and effort; but it plays a significant part in the development of Christlikeness. We must remember that God is more interested in our being increasingly like His Son than He is in our always doing what appears to us most beneficial.

SUMMARY AND CONCLUSION

The broader questions of just how God leads His children, what decisions are ours to make, and what is involved as we seek to make wise decisions are not our topic. Others have discussed the problem of guidance at length and have done an admirable job of examining the biblical principles.[5] We may now turn to other aspects of the problem of mysticism. But before we leave this topic, it may be well to stress again the fact that if we hold to the traditional view that God directs us through inner impressions, we have little defense against mystical origins for doctrine as well. We unwittingly give credence to much of the heresy that is being propagated by the various cults that flourish today. We have opened the gates to every kind of heresy, precisely because we have rejected in practice the view that the Scriptures alone are the final source and test of all truth.

5. Ibid.

6

THE EXAMPLE OF MYSTICISM:
Voice of Misdirection

We have seen in chapter 2 that certain doctrinal concepts that appear harmless, notably the distinction often made between "head" and "heart" knowledge, are not as innocuous as they may appear. In this case, as well as in some other parallels, a psychological theory is implied about man that is contrary to what the Bible teaches. If our view of man is wrong, then much of our theology will be distorted. Our beliefs about ourselves, salvation, and the Christian life will all be affected. But how significant are such distortions? Are they important enough that they deserve the degree of attention we are giving them here? Because of widely held viewpoints presently flourishing in new religions in the West, I believe they are.

MISDIRECTED PHILOSOPHY OF EDUCATION

Watchman Nee, a Chinese Christian who died in 1972 in a communist prison camp in China, is described by Dana Roberts as "one of the most popular contemporary theologians."[1] Nee's writings have exerted a great deal of influence in evangelical circles.

> A man of immense ability as a preacher and writer, his ministry was not hindered during his twenty-year incarceration for being an apolitical and independent religious leader. No longer in the position to preach openly, his messages were published before his death in over thirty volumes in many languages. Through the printed media his books continue to influence the interpretation of the Bible within the global evangelical movement.[2]

Watchman Nee has been, and still is, held in high esteem as a spiritual leader with deep insight. Yet his theological position is deeply mystical. Roberts is certainly correct when he says, in the passage quoted above, that Nee's books continue to influence the interpretation of the Bible in evangelical circles. Unfortunately, they have been a significant force in the growing mysticism in evangelical circles, precisely because they do influence the way many interpret the Bible. However, rarely does one hear a voice of caution when Nee is mentioned. In fact, I find many sincere Christians shocked and offended when I suggest that Nee's writings should be read and scrutinized carefully for major errors. Yet, as we shall see directly, Nee is often far from the mark. Nor is his mystical theology innocuous. It has already born some tragic fruit.

There is currently abroad in the United States a teaching that is growing rapidly, largely by drawing members from evangelical groups. This movement should be of special interest to us here for several reasons. First, it has grown by drawing people who already claim to be Chris-

1. Dana Roberts, *Understanding Watchman Nee* (Plainfield, N.J.: Logos International, 1980), p. ix.
2. Ibid., p. ix.

tians. Second, many of its teachings are far from biblically correct, yet they grow directly from Watchman Nee's position. Finally, the foundation upon which the erroneous mystical views rest is that same mistaken view of man we discussed earlier.

Although there is much that is unscriptural in this teaching, I intend to concentrate on what I believe to be a root source for most of the other errors: the view of revelation. Adherents deny that the Bible is God's completed and sufficient revelation to man, insisting that it only *contains* revelation for those who can pierce through the words to gain the true "meaning" behind them—a meaning that is not conceptual at all. How they arrive at this conclusion we will examine in a moment. First, however, we should remind ourselves of something that is basic to historic Protestant Christianity, including evangelicalism.

Scripture alone is seen as the final authority, because it alone, of all written or spoken statements, is the revelation of God. This has both positive and negative implications. First, it means that the written Word of God is the final criterion by which all claims to truth must be tested. Although there are many elements of nonbiblical information that may be important to us (for example, that radioactive materials may be dangerous to our health), any interpretation of a fact that contradicts clear scriptural teaching must be rejected as false. In other words, this claim is not that the Bible contains all true information, but rather that all information it does contain is true.

Second, to say that Scripture and Scripture alone is the final authority is to say that anything that claims authority equal to the Bible is making a false claim. We have no right to attribute to God doctrine that is not contained in His Word. Hence, such extrabiblical views are not binding on us. We are morally bound to obey only the Word, but not the ordinances of men unless these fall under the biblical admonition to be subject to those "higher powers" ordained of God.

Finally, implicit in the Bible-supreme principle is the claim that, although some knowledge of God is possible through nature (Rom. 1:18-20), the bulk of knowledge of spiritual things is gained through the written Word. Further implications include two thoughts: the mind is the indispensable, divinely ordained tool of spiritual growth; and revelation (in the theological sense of new information from God) is already complete in the Scriptures.

All this lies at the heart of Protestant Christianity and is involved in the claim that the Bible is the final authority in matters of doctrine. It is tragic that many Christians fail to realize the centrality of this issue. Because of this blind spot, they are vulnerable to some of Satan's most successful attacks on their faith.

On the basis of Watchman Nee's views concerning the nature of man, some groups will deny that the Scriptures are the sole revelation of God. Instead they insist that since the Spirit of God dwells in the spirit of man, God communicates directly with man. Thus we can receive direct revelation from God.

As we have already seen, Protestant Christianity has always (at least until quite recently) denied this kind of truth claim. Here, again, there is serious confusion among Christians regarding "revelation" and "illumination." Revelation is God's giving new information to man about Himself or about His universe. Thus, because God created the universe and mankind in a certain way, we are able to learn about God's "eternal power and divine nature" by examining ourselves and the rest of His creation (Rom. 1:18-20). This is called "general revelation." When creation was finished this kind of revealing was completed, although its edifying effect continues through the ages.

But when God chose to speak more specifically to mankind, He selected prophets and apostles as His instruments. By them God revealed conceptual information in propositional form. This act of God is called "special revelation." Protestantism has always insisted that this revelation was completed when the writing of the Bible was finished.

Completed revelation does not mean that God is uninvolved in what happens in the present. The Holy Spirit is actively involved in helping us to understand the Word when we read it or hear it read. This is not revelation, but rather illumination. It is God's continuing work in the mind of the hearer of the Word, whereby He helps him to grasp the actual meaning of what He said long ago through the apostles and prophets.

Any denial, on the other hand, that the Bible is the completed revelation of God implies that God is continuing to communicate with man now as He did in the time of the writing of the Bible. This, of course, results in the position that this present-day revelation is authoritative in a way equal to or superior to the Scriptures. Actually, such a position often is tantamount to insisting that such current revelation is significantly superior to the written Word. After all, if it is truly God who is speaking to us, how can it be anything but authoritative? And if what He is now saying to us is different from what He said to Moses or Peter long ago, how do we dare to reject His present statement in favor of an old and obviously outdated earlier statement? Consequently, such a view must finally result in the position that current revelation is superior to the written Word. And this is exactly what some are teaching today.

However, they do not teach that God speaks to individuals in language that can be rationally understood. Rather, this "revelation" is in our spirits and is a mystical experience, rather than something grasped by the mind. It is a direct, immediate revelation, not mediated through the written Word. Ordinary knowledge of all kinds is scorned as inferior and unspiritual because it depends on the mind. On the other hand, that which is non-rational is praised as spiritual.

Many Christians fail to see that God's revelation is in propositional form. It is in language comprehendible only with the mind. This fact proves that the redeemed mind is God's chosen tool for relating to man. Thus, rather than rejecting rational processes, we should act as good stewards of His gracious provision of rationality. In humility we should seek to develop our mental abilities to their greatest capacity. The anti-intellectual attitude one often finds among Christians is not spiritual but is instead dishonoring to God.

MISDIRECTED DOCTRINE OF MAN

I have said that these tragic and clearly unscriptural views are the direct result of Watchman Nee's teachings. To understand how such an unfortunate position is arrived at we must examine Nee's erroneous view of man, or, as I have chosen to call it, his psychology. As I will show, this psychological theory is not drawn from Scripture, but rather is forced onto it. Once the Bible is read from this position it is understood to say what it does not really say at all.

If I am correct in saying that Nee's theory of man is unbiblical, it is not surprising that the results would be serious. Falsehood is always dangerous. "But," someone may object, "how can Nee's position be said to be unbiblical? He sounds so spiritual and is respected by seemingly mature evangelical leaders. Surely he is not wrong."

A quote from Nee's *The Release of the Spirit* will serve to acquaint us with his position in his own words:

When God comes to indwell us, by His Spirit, Life, and power, He comes into our spirit which we are calling the inward man. Outside of this inward man is the soul wherein functions our thoughts, emotions and will. The outermost man is our physical body. . . . We must never forget that our inward man is the human spirit where God dwells, where His Spirit mingles with our spirit.[3]

It is important to notice that Nee here distinguishes three parts to man, something that is not unusual in itself. In fact, this division of man into body, soul, and spirit can be found rather clearly in Scripture. What is puzzling is that Nee then sets out to do what the biblical writers nowhere attempt to do, namely, to define each of the latter two "parts." We should notice that Nee clearly sees the spirit as something distinctly different from either the mind, the will, or the emotions. These he calls the soul. On the other hand, in *The Spiritual Man*, Nee explains what he believes the spirit of man to be:

According to the teaching of the Bible and the experience of believers, the human spirit can be said to comprise three parts; or, to put it another way, one can say it has three main functions. These are conscience, intuition and communion. The *conscience* is the discerning organ which distinguishes right and wrong; not, however, through the influence of knowledge stored in the mind but rather by a spontaneous direct judgment. . . . *Intuition* is the sensing organ of the human spirit. . . . *Intuition* involves a direct sensing independent of any outside influence. That knowledge which comes to us without any help from the mind, emotion or volition comes intuitively. We really "know" through our intuition; our mind merely helps us to

3. Watchman Nee, *The Release of the Spirit* (Cloverdale, Ind.: Ministry of Life, 1965), p. 10.

> "understand". . . . *Communion* is worshiping God. The organs of the soul are incompetent to worship God. God is not apprehended by our thoughts, feelings or intentions, for He can only be known *directly* in our spirits. Our worship of God and God's communications with us are directly in the spirit. They take place in "the inner man," not in the soul or outward man.[4]

We should notice, then, that for Nee the spirit of man functions in a noncognitive, nonrational way. Its actions are mystical actions. Nee makes clear that it is the spirit that relates us to God, rather than the soul. "God is a Spirit. Our spirit alone is of the same nature as God."[5] "Our spirit is given to us by God to enable us to respond to Him. But the outward man is ever responding to things without, thus depriving us of the presence of God."[6] Thus, it is only through mystical activity that we relate to God. The mind has a place, but merely as a tool for the spirit. Man's rationality has value only when it is controlled by his spirit.

> Each element has its own particular use. The spirit is employed to know the heavenly realities. Now we are not trying to disparage the use of the soul's faculties. They *are* useful, but here they must play a *secondary* role. They should be under control and not be the controller. The mind should submit to the spirit's rule and should follow what intuition fathoms of the will of God.[7]

Notice that Nee is not saying that man's mind has value only when it is controlled by the Holy Spirit, but rather when it is controlled by his human spirit.

4. Watchman Nee, *The Spiritual Man* (New York: Christian Fellowship Publishers, 1968), 2:31-32.
5. Nee, *The Release of the Spirit*, p. 24.
6. Ibid., p. 25.
7. Nee, *The Spiritual Man*, 2:93.

In His dealing with man, God's Spirit never bypasses man's spirit. Nor can our spirit bypass the outer man. ... As the Holy Spirit does not pass over man's spirit in His working in man, no more does our spirit ignore the outward man and function directly. In order to touch other lives, our spirit must pass through the outward man.[8]

What is meant by being a spiritual man is that he is under the control of his spirit which has become the highest organ of his whole person.[9]

What, then, is Watchman Nee's position? Briefly stated, he claims that man consists of three parts: body, soul, and spirit. The soul consists of the mind (or intellect), the will, and the emotions. The spirit is something totally different from these, consisting rather of the conscience (which is seen as a nonintellectual aspect), intuition, and a capacity for fellowship with God. Without these nonrational elements we could not relate to Him. Implied in all this is the idea that God is not in any sense "mental." He is Spirit, and all spirit is noncognitive. Thus, all relationship to God is necessarily mystical.

It should be evident by now that Nee's view is a totally mystical picture of man and his relationship to God. If Nee is correct, the only conclusion we can draw is that Christianity is a form of mysticism. In fact he goes so far as to say that one who is not mystical is not a Christian: "Man's soulical faculties cannot perceive God: nothing else can be a substitute for intuition. *Except a man receives a new life from God and has his intuition resurrected, he is eternally separated from God*" (italics added).[10] Nee is wrong. But, unfortunately, some Chris-

8. Nee, *The Release of the Spirit*, pp. 32-33.
9. Nee, *The Spiritual Man*, 2:32-33.
10. Ibid., 2:83.

tian leaders have failed to see his error, possibly because of their own failure to understand Scripture adequately.

Although the Bible refers to man as having three parts, which it identifies as body, soul, and spirit, it never defines any one of these. So when Watchman Nee teaches that the soul is made up of the intellect, the will, and the emotions, he is saying something that the Bible does not say. Of course, the fact that the Scriptures are silent on this subject does not in itself prove Nee wrong.

The biblical writers use the terms *soul* and *spirit* interchangeably at times.[11] This fact should make us suspicious of any attempt radically to distinguish the soul from the spirit.

A careful examination of Scripture will reveal an interesting fact: although the Bible does refer to man as body, soul, and spirit, it makes little or nothing of the distinction between soul and spirit. In fact, there are only two biblical statements that refer to both soul and spirit. In 1 Thessalonians 5:23, Paul prays that the entire person, spirit, soul, and body, will be kept from sin. Nothing more is said about the various components of man. In the other reference we find a suggestion exactly opposite from what some seem to believe it implies. Hebrews 4:12 speaks about a dividing between soul and spirit, and compares this to a dividing between "joints and marrow." The point of the verse is not to suggest that such a division can easily be made. Rather, because the joints of the body are largely bone, and marrow is a part of bone, such a dividing is virtually impossible. Likewise any dividing between soul and spirit is practically impossible. However, the Word of God is so powerful that, were a division to be made between soul and spirit, as between bone and marrow, the Bible would be the only instru-

11. W. E. Vine, *An Expository Dictionary of New Testament Words* (Westwood, N.J.: Revell, 1940), pp. 54-55 and 62-64. Compare the way the two words *spirit* and *soul* are used in the New Testament.

ment for making that division. This is a rhetorical device for emphasizing the power of God's Word, not a statement that can be used to prove we are capable of distinguishing between soul and spirit, as Watchman Nee tries to do.

Misdirected Interpretation of Scripture

By now it should be clear that the source of Watchman Nee's psychological picture of man is certainly not the Bible. The constant emphasis in Scripture is on knowing God's Word, and then on doing what we know. There is not even a hint to suggest that we can know with anything other than our minds. Yet Nee insists that "to perform God's will a Christian needs simply heed the direction of his intuition"[12] and that "when the Holy Spirit discloses the matters pertaining to God He does so not to our mind nor to any other organ but to our spirit."[13] The Bible says nothing of man's having or needing an intuition to relate to God, and it certainly does not make the result of salvation a quickening or resurrection of some intuitive function. All these claims are foreign to God's Word. They are ideas that Watchman Nee needs, however, in order to develop his unique kind of mystical theology of the "deeper Christian life."

What Nee does is to draw on his own experience for the standard of the Christian life. Apparently, his experience has involved strong mystical elements. At least some of his claims are openly stated to rest on experience:

> Though we may muster many arguments against it, even overwhelming it with reason, nevertheless this inner small voice still insists that we are wrong. Such experiences inform us that our intuition, the organ for

12. Nee, *The Spiritual Man*, 2:74.
13. Ibid., 2:88.

the working of the Holy Spirit, is capable itself of distinguishing good from evil without any assistance from
the mind's observation and investigation.[14]

In his attempt to see the Bible through the grid of his own
experience, he begins to do something very strange to the
Scriptures themselves. To what degree his thinking has
influenced others to treat the Word of God in a similar
manner I cannot tell. However, unfortunately, other
evangelical leaders also occasionally abuse the Bible in
the same way.

Examples of Nee's unusual treatment of Scripture
are easy to find. In volume one of *The Spiritual Man* he
lists three groups of references he says show "that our
spirits possess the function of conscience . . . , the function of intuition (or spiritual sense), and the function of
communion (or worship)."[15] Whereas some of the verses
listed in the groups referring to conscience and worship
do indeed refer to these things, none of those that he
claims for intuition in any way speak of such a thing.
They refer instead to such things as being "fervent in
spirit" and the spirit's being willing, but there is no hint
of some nonrational, intuitive function.

Another significant case of Nee's interpretive approach appears in his little book *Spiritual Reality or Obsession*, where he says, "What is spiritual reality? 'God is
a Spirit, and they that worship Him,' says the Lord, 'must
worship in spirit and truth.' The word 'truth' means 'trueness' or 'reality.' "[16]

However, truth is not the same as reality, although
the two concepts are related. A true statement is one that
gives us some accurate information *about* reality. How-

14. Ibid., 2:75.
15. Ibid., 1:32-33.
16. Watchman Nee, *Spiritual Reality or Obsession* (New York: Christian Fellowship Publishers, 1970), p. 6.

ever, to claim that the two concepts are synonymous is to distort the meaning. If this were merely a slip or an unimportant point, then kindness would demand that it be ignored; unfortunately, it is neither. It is this misinterpretation of a key word that allows Nee to claim that much of what he wishes to teach in the rest of this book is in accord with Scripture when it is not.

However, disregard for the correct meaning of the biblical words chosen by the Holy Spirit is not the only problem apparent in Nee's handling of God's Word. At key points, instead of showing that his argument is biblical, Nee simply states that something is fact, totally without any scriptural evidence. This leaves the reader with only two choices: either accept the claim on Nee's authority alone, or else reject it. This allows Nee to make some very questionable claims, which the uncritical reader will tend to believe came from Scripture.

One example of such faulty interpretation will serve to show the dangerous direction this takes in Watchman Nee's writings:

> A wonderful thing happens after you touch reality. Whenever you encounter someone who has not touched, or entered into, reality, you immediately sense it. You know he has not touched that reality because he is still following the mind, the law, the rule or regulation. Before God there is something which the Bible calls "true." It is nothing other than "reality."In relating to this trueness—this reality—one is delivered from doctrine, letter, human thoughts, and human ways.[17]

What has Nee said? It is rather difficult to answer that question, mainly because he does not give us a clear definition of his word *reality*. However, several things stand out in this quote. He claims that the person who

17. Ibid., p. 13.

has "touched reality" now has the ability to sense things about others immediately. In this example what is sensed is that the other person has not "touched reality." From other examples in the same book we see that this "sensing" extends to other things as well. For example, something may not be as it appears when one man forgives another. "Now sometimes you see a brother forgiving another brother who has offended him. . . . Judging by outward appearance, he really forgives most generously; yet somehow you do not feel right inside."[18]

In *The Release of the Spirit*, this sensing ability is said to result from the "release" of our spirit. It is said to be something that happens when one has "touched reality." It is described as our spirit touching the spirit of the other person.

> Furthermore, we may most spontaneously contact the spirit in others by our spirit. Whenever one speaks in our presence, we can 'size him up'—evaluate what kind of person he is, what attitude he is taking, what sort of Christian he is, and what his need is. Our spirit can touch his spirit.[19]

Much could be said about these claims, most of it negative. But suffice it to point out that such activity is never taught in the Bible to be the proper function of all Christians. This ability is clearly not a cognitive one that involves judging by applying biblical principles. Rather, it is described as "feeling" without understanding why, a totally subjective, intuitive response.[20] Yet Nee claims that every Christian should experience the "release" of his spirit so that he will be able to touch the spirit of others. He sees it as a proper function to be sought. Again he

18. Ibid., p. 23.
19. Nee, *The Release of the Spirit*, p. 23.
20. Nee, *Spiritual Reality or Obsession*, pp. 14-15.

makes claims, not taught in Scripture, about what is proper for Christians.

There is another, even more serious, claim in the Nee quotation we've been discussing. He says that "in relation to this trueness—this reality—one is delivered from doctrine." Typically, the context does not make clear just what is meant by "doctrine." However, a statement made later seems to indicate that Nee means the teachings of Scripture, in other words, biblical doctrine.

> How very vain it is for man to act on the basis of doctrine, for all he has is nothing more than an outward conduct. He does not have the true article—the reality.
> Sometimes we are close to being false simply because we know too much and act according to doctrine, instead of following the leading of God's Spirit. Whenever we act on the basis of doctrine we are not touching reality.[21]

Nee does not say that we are wrong because we believe what is false. Rather we are wrong because we act on the basis of what we know and understand rationally. Therefore, whatever we do is wrong, not because the action itself is wrong, but because the action is not the result of the "release of the spirit" or of "touching reality." He who is what he should be before God is "delivered from doctrine." He no longer needs to concern himself with gaining rational knowledge of God's Word.

This is, of course, a typical mystical position. *Doctrine* implies a rational grasp of principles, an understanding by the mind of information about objective reality. Nee's radical separation between the soul and the spirit, between the rational and the intuitive, and his elevation of nonrationality requires just such a rejection of doc-

21. Ibid., pp. 27-28.

trine. It is interesting to notice that this rejection is occasioned by his own rational conclusions. Logic leads him to be consistent with his rejection of logic, which is something of a contradiction in itself. But in fairness to Watchman Nee, we remember that he does not totally reject the mind, but subjects it to the intuitive urges. The claim that reason should somehow be the servant of intuition or imagination is common among mystics.[22]

In insisting on a secondary place for doctrine, Nee is setting up a conflict between the written Word of God and what he takes to be the work of the Holy Spirit within us. Because according to him the Holy Spirit is indistinguishable from our spirit,[23] and because our spirit consists of noncognitive elements, therefore, Nee teaches, the work of the Holy Spirit within us does not have a cognitive dimension. However, Scripture is God's written Word, present in propositional form and available to us through the mind. Watchman Nee's position rejects the true significance of the Bible.

> We must recognize two very different ways of help before us. First, "there is a way that seemeth right" in which help is received from the outside—through the mind—by doctrine and its exposition.
>
> Second, we must see that God's way is the way of spirit touching spirit. Instead of having our mentality developed or acquiring a storehouse of knowledge it is by this contact that our spiritual life is built up. Let no one be deceived; until we have found this way we have not found true Christianity.[24]

22. Sheldon Cheney, *Men Who Have Walked with God* (New York: Dell, 1945), pp. xi-xii.
23. Nee, *The Release of the Spirit*, p. 20. Nee says, "One remarkable thing is that God does not mean to distinguish between his Spirit and our spirit." Nee is clearly wrong here. There is no biblical basis for this claim.
24. Ibid., p. 89.

Does Nee mean that knowledge of the Word of God that is not acted on is insufficient for spirituality? This is clearly not what he is saying, and the rest of his book makes this clear. He means just what he says: that he who is not functioning in this subjective, mystical, intuitive way he calls "spirit touching spirit" has not "found true Christianity." This same theme is emphasized over and over in *The Spiritual Man*. Notice, for example, the following statements:

> We do not sense God and the realities of God by our intellect; else eternal life would be meaningless.[25]

> To be led by the spirit is to follow its intuition. All spiritual knowledge, communion and conscience come via the intuition. The Holy Spirit leads the saints by this intuition. They need not themselves figure out what possibly is spiritual; all that is required is to abide by their intuition. In order to listen to the Spirit we must apprehend His mind intuitively.[26]

> Nothing else can be a substitute for intuition. Except a man receives a new life from God and has his intuition resurrected, he is eternally separated from God.[27]

In other words, true Christianity is a form of mysticism. The person who is not functioning on the basis of intuition is not a Christian.

The biblical teaching, on the other hand, is that the Holy Spirit's tool in doing His work in us is the written Word.[28] In fact, I find no basis in Scripture for suggesting

25. Nee, *The Spiritual Man*, 2:83.
26. Ibid., 2:133.
27. Ibid., 2:83.
28. For some biblical examples see John 17:17; Eph. 6:17; Col. 3:16; and 1 Pet. 1:23.

that He ever works in us apart from our knowledge of God through His creation or the written Word. The Scriptures know nothing of a tension between the written Word of God and the work of the Holy Spirit within us, as Nee suggests.[29]

MISDIRECTED ELEVATION OF MYSTICISM

We have, in a sense, come full circle. Nee's psychology leads him to give an deficient position to Scripture —a place in the life of the Christian that is inferior to that given it by the Bible itself. This explains to some degree the carelessness with which he treats scriptural statements. But this is just what we would expect from one who sees the mind as an element in man that is inferior to intuition in knowing and relating to God. His careless treatment of biblical statements, in turn, makes possible his claim that his view is scriptural, since such loose interpretation allows him to read into Scripture what he believes to be the truth and to "find" it there. This, then, frees him to use his own mystical experiences as the standard by which to judge what is proper in the Christian life.

Doubtless, Watchman Nee is sincere in his beliefs. I do not believe that he knowingly distorts biblical truth. Unfortunately, sincerity is not enough. If he is wrong as I have claimed, and if careful examination of Scripture reveals this error as clearly as I have implied, why would someone as capable, dedicated, and sincere as Watchman Nee not see the problem himself?

Any complete answer to that question is complex and outside the scope of our concerns here. However, one important fact is clear. Nee believes that the person whose spirit has been "released" has a unique, effortless

---

29. For a discussion of this point, see Jerram Barrs, *Shepherds and Sheep* (Downers Grove, Ill.: InterVarsity, 1983), pp. 27-38.

means for seeing the "true" or "hidden" meaning in Scripture.

> We touch the spirit of revelation in the Bible. Without effort we can use our spirit to receive divine revelation.[30]

> The world cannot understand that there is a spirit in God's Word, and that that spirit can be released just as it is manifested in prophetic ministry. Today if you are listening to a prophetic message, you will realize that there is a mystic something other than word and thought present. This you can clearly sense, and may well call it the spirit in God's Word.
> There is not only *thought* in the Bible; the *spirit itself* comes forth. Thus, it is only when your spirit can come out and touch the spirit of the Bible that you can understand what the Bible says.[31]

What is Nee saying? At least two distinct things are clear. First, one can receive direct revelation from God. It is not clear whether this is factual information with the authority of Scripture, but it seems doubtful that it is. Instead, it is probably some inner, subjective experience, not something cognitive. Of this "revelation" Nee says, "When God opens our eyes that we may know the intent of our heart and the deepest thought within us in the measure that He knows us—this is revelation."[32]

Second, there is the claim that the Bible has more to it than thought. There is also a "spirit." It is important to notice here that Nee is definitely not speaking of the Holy Spirit. Each time he refers to the Holy Spirit he either calls Him by that name or uses the capitalized personal pronoun, or capitalizes the word *spirit*. In this passage,

30. Nee, *The Release of the Spirit*, p. 23.
31. Ibid., pp. 52-53.
32. Ibid., p. 72.

he does none of these. What he means is something else, more closely related to the idea of a mood, something felt or sensed about the words. A biblical passage or a prophecy has about it what Nee calls a "mystic something." "This you can clearly sense," he says, "and you may call it the spirit in God's Word."[33] It is only by one's spirit "touching" this "spirit" that he can really understand what the Bible says.

What Nee is saying, in his own unique way, is not at all new. This is the old Gnostic idea that there is a hidden meaning in the Bible.[34] This hidden meaning is not discoverable by studying the words of Scripture. Instead, it is something discovered in a mystical way, through his "inner sensing." How does the Christian whose spirit has been "released," "test all things"? By this inner, subjective, "spirit-touching-spirit." How does Nee know he is right and others are wrong? By this same mystical test. With this, then, as the basis for determining the meaning of Scripture, it is easy to understand why Watchman Nee would fail to see the problem. From a mystical position, his view cannot be wrong.

Fortunately, Watchman Nee does not carry his position to its logical extension. He does not elevate his own pronouncements, based on these mystical elements, to an authoritative position equal to or greater than Scripture. However, he has clearly laid the foundation for such an equation. Others, however, have taken that inevitable step, as we saw earlier in this chapter. And it does seem inevitable that once we see our own inner states as the voice of God we should view them as having final authority. Then these urgings seem to us to be binding on us, and perhaps on others also.

33. Ibid.
34. Lucius Waterman, *The Post-Apostolic Age*, vol. 2 of *Ten Epochs of Church History*, ed. John Fulton (New York: Scribner's, 1898), p. 200.

The elevation of the subjective experience to the place of final authority occurs at nearly every level. When Watchman Nee speaks critically about one who is "still following the mind, the law, the rule or regulation," and says that he who has "touched reality" is freed from "doctrine, letter, human thoughts, and human ways," in the passage we quoted earlier, this can easily be seen to mean that one is freed from all moral principles that are not dictated to him by his own conscience. When he claims that the intuition alone, without "the mind's observation," is capable of distinguishing between good and evil, he is saying that we need not know the dictates of Scripture. Again, Nee does not himself go so far as to say so. He believes biblical principles are binding on us. However, he has laid the foundation; others have built on his position carrying it to its logical conclusion. They have taught that biblical precepts are binding only if, and when, they are in accordance with the dictates of one's own conscience. Since conscience is understood to operate totally on the basis of intuition, and to be the tool of the Holy Spirit in controlling our behavior, this results in the view that one may do anything that feels right. Some have gone so far as to maintain that God has told them to divorce their mates in order to marry someone else, in direct violation of clear biblical prohibitions against divorce.

This situation comes about, almost necessarily, from making inner urges and intuitions a source of authoritative truth. These inner factors have no independent criteria outside themselves by which they are to be tested. Then, when a conflict arises with the dictates of common sense, reason, or even Scripture, primacy is given to the mystical revelations. This takes on a special degree of legitimacy when one identifies these inner states with the Holy Spirit, as Nee does. Unfortunately, this tragic mistake is also made by a great number of other sincere Christians.

Examples of mystical elements in the writings of other evangelical individuals could be easily documented. Well-known evangelist and politician Pat Robertson has repeatedly referred to revelations he gets from God. These voices guide him in all his decisions, and he plans to continue obeying these messages in the future.

Richard Foster, author of several widely read books including *Celebration of Discipline,* although much more Bible-integrated than some authors, follows a somewhat ambiguous path when he writes of cultivating meditation and imagination in the effort to hear God's voice.

A. W. Tozer, famous preacher and author of the last generation, writes of "knowledge by direct spiritual experience" in his book *Man: The Dwelling Place of God.* For this kind of revelation, he asserts, "The possibility of error is eliminated."

These and numerous other Christian leaders have shown philosophical affinity for the mysticism of Watchman Nee even though their theological perspectives may be widely separated on other matters.

SUMMARY AND CONCLUSION

The key to Watchman Nee's position is: the nonrational, intuitive functions of man provide a special "organ" for relating to God.[35] Once this is accepted, the door is open for all sorts of nonbiblical views. If God speaks directly to us apart from the written Scriptures, then such inner speaking must be authoritative. The Scriptures are no longer the final authority.

We have examined the example of a respected author whose writings have had a profound influence in

35. Nee, *The Spiritual Man,* 1:32.

evangelical circles, even though his writings are danger-ously mystical. As such an important influence, Nee's position has been a major force toward mysticism in many groups. In the next chapter, the impact of mysticism on the charismatic movement will be demonstrated.

7

THE ZENITH OF MYSTICISM:
Charismatics in Christianity

The charismatic movement provides an interesting example of the influence of mystical thought in Christianity. Before we examine the ideas that underlie this movement, it will be well to clarify some important related issues.

CHARACTERISTICS OF THE CHARISMATIC MOVEMENT

What is now known as the "charismatic movement" is an interesting combination of attitudes, beliefs, and experiences shared by a large group of people from widely divergent backgrounds and denominations. There is a strong charismatic element within the Roman Catholic church. At the opposite end of the ecclesiastical spectrum from Roman Catholicism are some Protestant Pentecostal groups who are also charismatic. In fact, the charismatic movement is often called the "Neo-Pentecostal movement," because it shares so much with the older Pentecostal movement, even though there are important differences. Because the "charismatic experience" spans such widely different denominations, with historic positions that are often at odds, if not openly contradictory, it will be necessary to limit our consideration to that part of the movement that directly affects the evangelical churches.

But even with this understanding, the term *charismatic* means many different things to different people within evangelical circles. The reader should remember this semantical diversity when applying this term to individuals or groups. In the final analysis, it is not the labels by which we identify ourselves, but the beliefs we hold that matter most.

The term *charismatic* is derived from the Greek word *charisma*, which means "a gift of grace," referring to a gift that comes to us because of God's grace. Because *grace*, used in this sense, refers to God's "friendly disposition from which the kindly act proceeds . . . ,"[1] the word *charisma* speaks more clearly about the nature of the Giver than about the gift. However, the word *charismatic* has come to stand for those who emphasize these "spiritual gifts."

Another problem exists for anyone discussing this movement. There are, on the one hand, the theories or doctrines that underlie the movement and, on the other, the psychological dynamics of it. Sometimes movements originate in well-developed theories; sometimes they spring from psychological factors rather than from shared beliefs. In the case of the charismatic movement, both origins seem present. However, because ideas tend to separate people, it is the psychological roots that probably unite the charismatic people in this common movement despite their differences in theology.

The difficulty, then, is this: the explanation one person gives to justify his charismatic experience is often not shared by the next person, although some of the phraseology used may be common to both. A superficial

---

1. W. E. Vine, *An Expository Dictionary of New Testament Words* (Westwood, N.J.: Revell, 1940), pp. 146-47 and 169-70.

hearing given to both persons may lead a third party to think these two believe the same thing. A critical examination, however, exposes serious differences.

This difficulty is further complicated by the fact that the charismatic person often has little patience with theology. As a result, he has no clear doctrinal discernment. His ignorance may be masked, even from himself, by his ability to repeat the clichés that are widely shared in the movement. However, if he were asked to explain those phrases he may find himself largely at a loss for words.

The result of this doctrinal weakness is that any description of the underlying theory of the charismatic movement will be only partially correct, at best. It may be accurate for many, but will be sincerely disputed by others.

One occasionally hears charismatics make statements like "Doctrine divides; experience unites." Such statements express impatience with theory. Just what the quotation means by "doctrine" is not clear. Some seem to mean by the term only those concepts of any group that are not vital to Christianity. Others apparently have all areas of theology in mind. These latter cases pose an inconceivable problem for biblical Christians. That anyone could believe that religious experience can be both without doctrinal content and yet significant seems almost unimaginable, yet this is what such a viewpoint implies. Because the Scriptures make the mental acceptance of certain truths about our Lord a primary requirement for salvation, it is difficult to see how anyone could so totally reject doctrine.

The charismatic movement is indeed dependent upon certain psychological dynamics. When one lists all those psychological factors that are special to the charismatic movement, an interesting phenomenon becomes apparent. Inasmuch as those charismatics who concern us here are evangelical Christians, there is a major body of characteristics that are unique to them. John L. Sherrill, in *They Speak with Other Tongues*, quotes Dr. Henry Pitney Van Dusen of Union Theological Seminary as calling Pentecostals "a third, mighty arm of Christendom."[2] The other two "arms" are Catholicism and Protestantism. It is doubtful that those who share Pentecostal beliefs merit so great a distinction as Van Dusen gives them, but it is true that they are different from the main streams of Christendom. When one asks what the basis for the differences are, the answer must focus on the significance that charismatics give to their subjective experiences, a significance that makes the subjective experience as important, or more so, than intellectually grasped truth.

A major emphasis of the charismatics is the Holy Spirit. They see their good feelings as either experiences of the Spirit or gifts provided by the Spirit; as either actions performed by the Third Person of the Trinity or gifts bestowed by Him in the form of abilities. In regard to the "gift of prophecy," for example, when practiced in conjunction with "speaking in tongues," the teaching is that the Spirit speaks through the person, so that the message is directly from God without the intermediate agency of even the speaker's own mind. The ability to speak "with other tongues" is usually seen as an ability conferred upon the speaker by the Spirit, while the message given in the "tongue" is the direct communication of the Spirit. At other times, religious feelings are identified as the Spirit Himself.

MYSTICISM WITHIN THE CHARISMATIC MOVEMENT

That subjective nonrational experiences are given the greatest importance within charismatic circles is illustrated by the charismatic explanation of the gifts of

2. John L. Sherrill, *They Speak with Other Tongues* (Old Tappan, N. J.: Revell, 1964), p. 28.

tongues and prophecy. Both gifts, especially when used together, and coupled with the "gift of interpretation," are based on inner, noncognitive urges.

The "gift of tongues" is the practice of speaking an unknown "language." It is unknown in the sense that it has not been learned by the speaker. If he had learned it the tongue would not be a "gift," nor would its practice be a miracle. Nor does he now understand it. Most non-charismatic Christians agree thus far. The charismatic also believes that, ordinarily, tongues-speaking "happens" to a person while he is under certain psychological predispositions.

The one who "interprets" tongues-speaking does not interpret in the ordinary sense of the term. There is no word-for-word translation. In fact, the "interpreter" often does not even claim to understand what was spoken, but rather states what he believes the Holy Spirit has told him.[3]

It would be interesting to ask several key questions of those involved in interpretation of tongues. First, how did he experience the Spirit's telling him the message? Did he somehow hear it in words? Second, how does he know that it was, in fact, the Holy Spirit, and not an illusion, his own imagination, or even some demonic source? Finally, how does he know that this is actually what the tongues speaker said?

The answer one would expect to the third question is, of course, obvious. If it truly was the Holy Spirit who gave the meaning, then this must be what was spoken in the "tongue." God cannot lie. But how would the question about the source be answered? It would seem that in response the appeal would have to be to some psychological aspect of the experience. Any answer given would need to focus on the experience that proved "immediate-

3. Ibid., p. 24.

ly (that is, directly, without appeal to some intervening factor) that it was the Holy Spirit.'"[4] It is doubtful that any simpler response could be given, although a more complex one might be. In my own experience, such questions have usually prompted the suggestion that I have no faith, or that I refuse to believe the truth, or that "these things are spiritually discerned." The last suggestion implied that I was not spiritual. Such answers are not really answers at all. They avoid the issue.

Most tongues interpreters would not answer the first question by saying that they heard the Spirit speak to them in words, nor that they understood the speaker's words. Instead, they were "deeply impressed" that their interpretation was the true meaning. This, of course, is once more an appeal to the subjective, noncognitive impressions, the key characteristic of mysticism.

Another example of charismatic appeal to the mystical concerns a common test for truth. At one point in his letter to the Romans, Paul says that "the Spirit Himself bears witness with our spirit . . ." (Rom. 8:16).[5] From this one reference some have concluded that there is an inner feeling by which the "Spirit-filled" Christian is able to judge not only the truth of some statement, but also the inner truthfulness of other people. Their view is similar to that held by Watchman Nee and others. Several different persons, describing this experience in my hearing, called it a feeling or emotion. One described it as an inner "buzzer" that sounded either a harsh alarm when a person who was not right with the Lord entered the room or a pleasant sound when the person was in right relationship with God. The same thing, he said, happened

4. Ibid., p. 88.
5. It should be noticed that this is the only place in all Scripture that any spirit is ever said to "bear witness with" any other spirit, and here it refers only to our assurance of our relationship to God as His children. There is also nothing in the passage indicating that this activity of the Holy Spirit is experienced as an inner feeling. It could just as well be seen as a rational process.

when one heard or read a message. This inner alarm system is an infallible test of truth. This experience is described by these people as their own "spirit bearing witness." If another person is involved then it is "my spirit bearing witness with your spirit."

This same thing is present in Watchman Nee's writings. However, Nee, with his greater concern for explanation, has a well-developed psychology as the basis for such nonrational "sensing," a psychology that we conclude is unscriptural. In those charismatic groups that speak of "spirit bearing witness with spirit," a similar psychological theory seems to be assumed. However, considering the widespread influence of Watchman Nee's writings, it is not unreasonable to suggest that he may be the source of this view. Roberts, in discussing the influence of Nee on the charismatic movement in *Understanding Watchman Nee*, says, "Apart from theologians within the movement itself, one of the most widely read theologians is Watchman Nee."[6]

This mystical test of truth demonstrates that several individuals, each using similar terms, may not agree about what is involved. Some say that what we have just described is a direct activity of the Holy Spirit Himself, the "voice" of the Spirit. Others insist that it is the person's own spirit, sensitized by the Holy Spirit. Watchman Nee and others would ascribe it to the person's own spirit once it is "released." In any case, here is a clear example of a mystical experience identified as the work of God.

Because of the charismatic explanation of "tongues," "prophecy," and "interpretation," it is easy to see the emphatic role of mysticism within this movement. Much of what is identified by charismatic brothers as "gifts of the Spirit" is mystical and provides major problems for

6. Dana Roberts, *Understanding Watchman Nee* (Plainfield, N.J.: Haven, 1980) p. xi.

one who wishes to be true to the Word of God. Whereas our purpose is not primarily to examine the charismatic movement as a whole, one more example will be sufficient to show the problems one faces if he claims he has, in this case, the "gift of prophecy."

Many difficulties arise when a subjective urge, identified as God's revelation, is not open to any public test of truth. The subjective factor is itself without rational content and therefore cannot properly be called either true or false. It just "is." To say something is either true or false is to imply that it has rational content. The words *true* and *false* apply properly only to propositions. If someone claims to have a "word from God" and that "message" was not given in words, then the "prophet" has interpreted it during the articulation process. This interpretation is the "prophet's" judgment of what the impression meant. How does he know that this is what the urge means? Perhaps even more significantly, how are we, who have not had the impression, to test whether or not his interpretation is correct?

Another difficulty concerns the source of the message. How is anyone, the "prophet" himself or his hearers, to determine if the source of that prophecy was really God? Might it not just as well have been his own desires, the effect of a physical disorder, some psychological quirk, or even "the father of lies"? What test is available? If the experience was truly nonrational, without cognitive content, no test seems to apply, not even the test of Scripture itself. And we must keep in mind that we are commanded to "test the spirits" (1 John 4:1).

But let us suppose that the "prophet" maintains that the message came to him in clear words, or in some way so that, although the choice of the exact words was his own, the concepts were absolutely clear. The message, then, would be cognitive and with rational content. There are still problems, however, if we wish to deal with the issue as intelligent, informed Christians who take the Bible seriously.

In order to see these further problems and in order to be fair to the issues and to the people involved, we must mention a possible distinction between two different uses for the word *prophecy*. This distinction will be developed later. For now we begin by recognizing that God wishes to control every aspect of our being (Rom. 12:1-2, 8:5-8). This includes our minds. When He is in control of what we think, then our thoughts could be said to be "from God." This control is never total, so as to strip us of effort or responsibility, nor does it eliminate the possibility of error. Therefore, it is not wise to say that what we believe to be true is "from God." Such a statement might lead someone to believe our beliefs came by direct revelation. "Direct revelation" is a message from God provided in such a way that man is not responsible for its content and the very possibility of error is removed. This second kind of "speaking for God" is genuine prophecy, not the first.

How, then, is someone who wishes to be true to Scripture to deal with the claims of those who insist they speak for God in this mystical way? The problem concerns whether or not a message said to be a "prophecy from God" is to be believed. Unfortunately, it is not as simple a situation as such a statement makes it appear. It is not simply a question of believing or not believing the message. The claim consists of several components, each of which is actually an issue in its own right.

First, there is the implication that God has spoken directly to the "prophet." Now, it might be tempting to say that the entire issue rests on this claim. If God has indeed spoken directly to this individual, and given this message, then we are obligated to believe it. If, however, God has not spoken, we should reject it. Certainly, we should believe whatever God has said, but should we re-

ject whatever God has not directly spoken? There are
many significant truths that we emphatically believe
which have not been directly spoken by God. It could be
that the content of a supposed prophetic message is true,
although the claim that God had spoken it in this *direct*
way to the prophet is false. If this were the case, then we
ought to still believe the message while rejecting the
claim to direct revelation. This is because we ought always to believe the truth from whatever source it may
come.

On the other hand, it is tempting to treat the matter
as though the truth of the message is the entire issue.
Why not judge the entire issue on only this as some of my
friends do? If the message, they say, does not contradict
the Scriptures, then we are safe in believing the message
without regard for anything else. This, however, ignores
some serious problems. Many important issues simply
are not addressed directly in Scripture. For example,
suppose that someone claimed that God had directly revealed to him the name of the particular person a congregation should call as its pastor. Certainly nothing in the
Bible is directly contradicted by such a message, yet the
choice of this man might prove most unfortunate if he
should fail. Yet, if the members of the congregation accepted such a message as being directly from God, without any other basis for their choice, they would be
obligated to call the designated person. If, however, they
based their decision on several considerations, they
would thereby be showing that they did not accept the
claim that the message was directly from God. At least
their actions would show that they believed such a claim
must be tested by other factors. This again raises the
question of the proper test, because here is an issue to
which the test of direct scriptural pronouncement does
not apply. How, then, are we to determine our attitude
toward the individual who claims to be God's "prophet"?

The answers most often given, when the discussion reaches this point, have several characteristics. The answers no longer are clearly based on Scripture, as though we are now free to turn elsewhere for truth on topics not found in the Bible. The answers also seem based on pragmatic considerations. The consideration given greatest importance seems to be the speaker's idea of what is most significant. The problem here is not that pragmatic considerations have no place, but rather we turn away too quickly from Scripture. When we consider these other factors we are not sufficiently committed to the supremacy of the Word in general, nor do we perceive the implications of our own beliefs about the proper priority of the Word.

Prophecy in the Charismatic Movement

The questions we must address at this point are: Should we expect direct communication from God to individual people? Are the Scriptures the complete and sufficient revelation of God? Most Christians who accept such direct, personal revelation do so, they say, because the gift of prophecy is listed among the gifts of the Spirit. This position uncritically assumes that the word *prophecy* has only one meaning. Is it true that this word always necessarily refers to direct communication by God to individual men apart from the vehicle of the written Word? This is clearly not the case. Some of what is called prophecy in the Scriptures is rather the application of what was already written to the current situations.[7] Many

---

7. The word translated *prophecy* ". . . signifies the speaking forth of the mind and counsel of God . . . " (W. E. Vine, *An Expository Dictionary of New Testament Words* (Westwood, N.J.: Revell, 1940), p. 221). Biblical prophets certainly spoke the direct message of God. They also spoke for God on the basis of what He had previously spoken. For one example, see Moses' message to Israel (Deut. 29:2ff). Also, notice that in the New Testament the entire Old Testament is called "the Law and the Prophets" (Luke 16:16, Rom. 3:21). This even includes the historical records of such books as Genesis.

times it involved no claim to *new* direct communication from God.

Understanding God's past direct communication, and recognizing how His written Word applies to the present situation is not a mechanical process. It is one that certainly demands the unique involvement of God's Spirit giving us insight. Consequently, this ability is clearly a gift of the Spirit. That the New Testament writers also used the term *prophecy* occasionally to mean direct revelation from God is quite true. However, when prophecy is listed among the spiritual gifts its meaning there does not necessarily refer to direct revelation. It may refer to the application of God's already revealed truth. To uncritically assume only one meaning in such listings is totally unjustified. This is a very important point to keep in mind. Furthermore, it is also clear from New Testament usage that much of the time when prophecy is mentioned the more general meaning is clearly in view.

The question still to be decided is, Are direct revelations ever to be expected now? This question has interesting ramifications. Considering how the New Testament was written, we would not expect to find a statement to the effect that direct revelation would cease with the death of the apostles. This is because the New Testament developed in the form of separate books and letters written over a period of time by a number of different authors that were later assembled into one collection. The question of the duration of God's special-revelation outreach to mankind is not directly addressed. For example, there is no passage that explicitly states that God's direct-revelation process would cease. However, evangelical Bible scholars have always and unanimously maintained that a strong case for such a position can be made from *indirect* scriptural evidence (e.g., Deut. 4:2, 12:32; Prov. 30:6; Rev. 22:18).

But if, after examining all relevant issues, we were to conclude that there is no adequate basis for believing that direct revelation has ceased, then we must recognize an important fact. The New Testament writers considered the Old Testament to be Scripture, their entire Bible, authoritative and binding upon them. They were consciously writing within that context. The Old Testament had within it clear guidelines for judging whether an alleged direct revelation is from God or not. There were also some firm tests both for the person who claims to be a prophet as well as for his message (Deut. 13:1-5; 18:20-22). These were never canceled or set aside in the New Testament. Some New Testament tests were added to those already in effect. These neither superseded nor abrogated the earlier tests out of the Old Testament.

In Old Testament times a person who claimed to speak for God was required to go through a process of proving to his contemporaries that he had indeed been chosen by God as His spokesman. The proof consisted of two parts, the first involving the correct prediction of some future event or some other miraculous sign. Only after this was done were people obligated to receive the prophet's message. Second, the message also had to be checked against already revealed written truth. The prophetic credentials of both Christ and His apostles were established in these ways. Jesus constantly showed how His teaching properly integrated with the Old Testament; His doctrine was not in conflict with Moses. His life and message were the fulfillment of the law. This was also true of the apostles.

Although, because the issue is not raised, it is not possible to prove from the biblical text that the prophetic credentials were evident in every person described in the New Testament as a prophet, we can see a similar pattern in some cases. In Acts 11:27-28 Agabus accurately predicts a famine, which took place during the reign of Claudius. Whether or not Agabus had previously made correct predictions we are not told, but that seems likely because he and his companions are called prophets. Apparently, they held that office in the sense that they functioned with some regularity in prophetic capacity. In view of the Old Testament regulations, had Agabus's prediction not come true he would have been discredited and no future claim of his to speak for God would have been accepted.

A principle now becomes clear. If it is true that God still does speak directly to certain gifted persons in the way He did in biblical times, and if we wish to be true to the Word, we must apply the prophet-testing structure developed in the Old and New Testaments. On the other hand, if some individuals or congregations are unwilling to apply these tests they have no right to claim that any man or message is directly from God.

These tests are objective and public. They involve careful rational evaluation by persons other than the alleged prophet. The tests are not private or subjective. They do not include "spirit bearing witness with spirit" or any intuitive "sensing" of the truth. A mystical approach is not even suggested. In fact, mysticism is almost necessarily ruled out by the demand for public and rational evaluation.

It must be emphasized that speaking for God is not a light matter. God's command to Israel was that anyone who claimed to speak for Him, but through whom He had not really spoken, was to be put to death. They were to be examined by the prescribed tests (Deut. 18:20-22). A similar, but broader, caution is issued in the New Testament. James tells us that "not many of you should presume to be teachers . . . because you know that we who teach will be judged more strictly" (James 3:1, NIV*). This is a warning that many seem to take far too lightly.

---

*New International Version.

Thus far we have been considering the problem of assuming that when the New Testament speaks of the "gift of prophecy" it is speaking of the imparting of information from God without the involvement of the written Word or of the human mind. Is such an assumption justified? It seems there is no biblical basis that leads us to that position. There is, moreover, a great deal of circumstantial evidence that would also say we are not justified in this assumption. This circumstantial evidence, though convincing, is neither conclusive in itself, nor is it drawn directly from Scripture.

First, it seems that from the earliest times the church has held that direct revelation from God was complete and had ceased with the death of the twelve apostles and their companions, who had personally witnessed our Lord's ministry, death, and resurrection. Here, the gift of prophecy is thought to be an apostolic gift. It is partly for this reason that the doctrine of the apostolic succession developed in the medieval church. Only by this doctrine could the apostolic authority of the bishops, and later of the pope, be defended. It was thought that only if the pope were in some sense an apostle would his claim to speak prophetically for Christ be justifiable. Consequently, the development of this Catholic doctrine may be seen as a kind of confirmation of the historic Protestant view that direct revelations from God were not to be expected except through one of the apostles.

One may argue that even if belief in final revelation in Scripture is historically traceable to the church's beginning, the church may have been mistaken all along. The simple fact that something is fervently and widely believed does not prove that it is true. However, the burden of proof rests on the one who rejects the orthodox view. Consequently, if it is true that the church has from the first believed in completed revelation, then someone claiming that God continues to speak revelationally to people should not expect others to believe his allegation unless he first shows convincing evidence that the church has been wrong all along. In the absence of such evidence, I find it hard to believe that some evangelical Christians accept the concept of continued direct revelation.

A further consideration involves the Protestant Reformation. The heart of that movement was the doctrine of *sola Scriptura*—the claim that Scripture alone is the authority for faith and practice. This doctrine demands, among other things, the total rejection of the Roman Catholic clergy's claim to direct revelations from God apart from the written Word. If we now believe that God has, does, or will speak to anyone today, we reject the heart of the Reformation.

The medieval Roman Catholic church was much more careful in using the claimed prophetic office than most present-day, self-proclaimed prophets have been. Yet in spite of that restraint, a great body of unbiblical theology had developed in Catholicism. Most of those teachings did not appear to contradict the Scriptures as viewed by the uncritical scholar. For example, the doctrine of purgatory certainly is not specifically denied in any biblical statement. We, of course, argue that Scripture does contradict purgatory doctrine wherever it rejects salvation by human merit, the foundational concept on which this Catholic teaching is based. However, this kind of argument involves more subtlety than most modern believers in "prophecies" are prone to grasp.

One final thought needs to be considered. When one studies church history it is interesting to note how regularly heresy has found its source in a claim to special revelation. A great many of the modern cults that thrive in the West have at their base someone's claim to be a "prophet." This should make evangelicals very cautious about accepting the belief that the New Testament gift of prophecy functioning today is the receiving of direct information from God.

All this is circumstantial evidence against the claim that God still speaks to people today in the same way that He spoke in biblical times. However, in the absence of positive biblical proof to the contrary, I think that the circumstantial evidence we have mentioned is highly significant.

There is a point in all this that is vitally at issue in charismatic groups. There is a contradiction involved in saying that information has been received by direct revelation from God and then in saying that the truthfulness of the new revelation is to be judged by men. If we already know that the God who cannot lie has truly spoken it, then we already know absolutely that it is true. Why should one evaluate it as though it might be false? By what authority dare a mere man sit in judgment upon it?

If, however, we judge such a message false or inaccurate we say that God has not spoken, or God is mistaken, or the messenger has confused the message. In each case, the prophet stands condemned.

If, on the other hand, we are dealing merely with human judgments, advice, or suggestions, and not with direct messages from God, the situation is quite different. No man in his right mind would claim that his view is above error or that it is always the wisest possible position. We know that, as humans, our knowledge is limited and fallible. Therefore, even if we believe that our advice is according to God's Word and we are speaking from a mind controlled by the Holy Spirit, there is room for error. If our message is judged to be less than all it should be, we are not condemned as we would be if we claimed the thought was from God.

It seems, however, that often the gift claimed by charismatics is either seen as guaranteeing the absolute trustworthiness of the message, or else the message is seen as open to tests of truth applied by others. If the gift guarantees the trustworthiness of the message then the message is equal in authority to the Holy Scriptures. On the other hand, to say that the message should be tested by men is a contradiction if one also maintains that it has come directly from God.

RESPONSES TO THE CHARISMATIC MOVEMENT

Where, then, does all this leave us? How should an intelligent evangelical Christian who seeks to be true to the Bible respond to the claim that some message is a direct revelation from God? First, the message should itself be rejected if it is in any way opposed to the Scriptures. The content of the message should be accepted if it agrees with the Bible. We should suspend judgment when we cannot determine whether or not it harmonizes with the Word.

The claim that the "prophet" is delivering a message given directly to him by God, and that it is not merely his understanding of something already found in the written Word, should first be judged on the basis of available evidence. If we decide that the evidence does not warrant rejecting the claim that prophecy continues, then we should ask about the prophet's credentials in accordance with the Old Testament structure. If he has not passed the appropriate tests at some time in the past, we have no obligation to accept his claim to speak for God.

This testing process involves a control situation that is not always possible. It requires that both the "prophet" and his critics be members of the same community of believers. This group should test the prophet within its own boundaries so that the members have themselves seen the evidence of his prophetic office. People are not obligated to believe someone when he claims to speak for God if they have no basis for believing him. Neither are they obligated to believe him on the basis of someone else's testimony whose personal trustworthiness they do not know.

It may be enlightening to ask what purpose phrases like "Thus saith the Lord" serve in the delivery of modern "prophecies." The purpose seems to be twofold, although both elements need not always be present. First, this phraseology may be intended to indicate that God's special message is involved. It lends authority to the message and encourages belief. Who would dare to reject the direct word of God Himself? These phrases will also serve to dissuade the hearers from disputing the wisdom of the prophecy.

Second, to say "Thus saith the Lord" serves to shift the responsibility from the speaker to God. Thus, if the message is unpleasant, the speaker cannot himself be held responsible. These purposes may not necessarily be the conscious motives of one who claims to be God's prophet. However, they should be recognized as possible explanations by both the person who speaks and those who listen.

On the whole, then, it seems to me that the entire issue of modern "prophecies" is open to question and fraught with uncertainty. The least we can say is that a great deal more study and consideration must be devoted to the subject before evangelical Christians approve such proclamations. At present, the evidence seems strongly against viewing the issue positively.

We have now briefly examined some of the problems a person faces who accepts Scripture as the final authority and who also wishes to accept the view that God's direct revelation is not finalized within the pages of the written Word. We should notice, however, that if any self-proclaimed prophet bases his message on a mystical experience or way of "knowing," then all of the problems inherent in mysticism are also present. If his message came through some nonconceptual inner impression, and not in the form of clear words, then it was a mystical experience. As such, it seems to have nothing in common with what the prophets and apostles of biblical times experienced and therefore it cannot be supported by the biblical text. The foregoing characterization seems to be typical of the charismatic experience.

What, then, are we to say of the charismatic movement? There has been much debate, both pro and con. Unfortunately, both sides have often been off target. The criticism, all too often, is limited to two areas: the embarrassing emotionalism that is so often present in the "exercise of the gifts"; and the question concerning whether or not the sign gifts of healing, tongues, and prophecy have ceased for the present age.

The objections having to do with the emotionalism are often matters of personal preference. The one who objects does so on the basis that he is embarrassed by such an open display of emotions. If this is nothing more than the personal preference of the critic, it is an unconvincing criticism. Others obviously do not share his discomfort. It may be grounds for not worshiping with that group, but that alone is no reason for the group to change its practices.

If, on the other hand, the emotionalism is believed to be the actual expression of the work of the Holy Spirit and is, therefore, somehow essential to the worship itself, then it probably is a form of mysticism and deserves to be rejected on that basis.

The second area of criticism is much more weighty. Are the alleged miracle gifts of the charismatics really a continuation of the New Testament gifts? Didn't the gifts terminate long ago?

The question concerning whether or not the sign-gifts have ceased is an important question of biblical doctrine. However, that question is not relevant to the present charismatic question if what these groups practice are not actually the biblical sign-gifts. For example, are the "gift of tongues" and the "gift of healing" as practiced today really what was practiced in the New Testament church? It seems doubtful that they are.

The scope and topic of this book make it unwise to attempt to support fully the negative conclusion just stated. However, it will be useful to consider a few facts. When Christ and the apostles performed healings, no one questioned their genuineness. On the other hand, it is clear from most of the references to speaking in tongues as practiced by the apostles that they were speaking known languages, not some kind of ecstatic utterances. All attempts to prove that some "language of angels" was being spoken, or that one should practice a "prayer language," are based on dubious biblical scholarship and therefore, on careful examination of the text, fail.

On close examination, these theological questions, as important as they are, are really not what is at issue. The important concern is that these "gifts," as often practiced, are expressions of an underlying mysticism. They occur in response to the belief that the work of the Holy Spirit in us is private, subjective, and noncognitive. Once these "spiritual experiences" occur they are then used as evidence of the Spirit's involvement. They become at once the grounds and the evidence for the correctness of mystical theology.

It is no secret that the charismatic movement as a whole tends to look with disfavor on scholarship. This springs from the fact that those who trust mystical experiences almost inevitably distrust the human mind. This, of course, leads to a deficiency in careful biblical analysis, which, in turn, prevents the identification of the error of mysticism. A vicious circle results. Error prevents study; lack of study prevents the discovery of the error.

If we fail to identify and confront the mysticism underlying charismatic phenomena we will never solve the theological problems. Most people, once absorbed with their own subjective experiences, will not break away from a mystical theology. In trying to challenge charismatic thinking, we will find ourselves vainly and constantly trying to counteract the *fruit* until we deal with the mystical *root* from which it grows.

One final thought should be mentioned before we leave the subject of the charismatic movement. As in all forms of mystical theology, the charismatic is unclear about what it means to be "a spirit." In this case, the difficulty expresses itself as an ambiguity. Evangelicals who are charismatic speak of the Holy Spirit as a Person, the Third Person of the Trinity. But they seem to forget His personhood when they think of how we relate to Him and how He relates to us. Both in the way they behave and in the way they speak of their relationship to God, they treat the Holy Spirit as though, being spirit, He is a feeling or mood. Or He is something to which one must relate primarily by means of feelings.

This is similar to the error in Watchman Nee, in which he described "spirit touching spirit." His view, of course, was that the spirit of man is the intuitive ability, the conscience, the ability to fellowship with God. He saw the human spirit as noncognitive in nature. By separating these from the mind, emotions and will, as he did, and by claiming that "our spirit alone is of the same nature as God,"[8] Nee has clearly implied that God is also noncognitive in nature and can be known only through nonrational, subjective urges. This same kind of confusion is present in charismatic teaching.

The view that God is a nonrational Being who uses noncognitive means to communicate with us, seems clearly mistaken because God has chosen to relate to us through the written Word. Furthermore, in all our experi-

8. Nee, *The Release of the Spirit*, p. 24.

ence of relating to other persons we do so primarily through rational interaction. We speak. The subjective aspects of all our interpersonal relationships begin with and depend on verbal, rational communication. To see God as a Being to whom we relate only subjectively is to deny to Him that very Personhood that is the basis of all significant relationship.

SUMMARY AND CONCLUSION

In conclusion, then, it seems that those factors of the charismatic movement that define it and set it apart from other groups and movements are either mystical themselves or result from elements that are mystical. The exact source of that mysticism is complex. I have suggested three possible explanations: first, poor biblical scholarship; second, a false view of what spirit is, specifically what the Holy Spirit of God is like; and finally, an inherent mysticism—that is, an inclination to give excessive significance to the inner "senses."

8

THE BORDERLINE OF MYSTICISM:
Relationship with God

In discussing mystical tendencies in evangelical thought with Christian friends, I find them expressing uncertainty and concern about two related areas: the ministry of the Holy Spirit in their lives and what they call their "personal relationship" to God. These areas still need to be addressed lest a misunderstanding remain.

RELATING TO GOD: CLARIFICATIONS

In various ways my evangelical friends indicate a fear of what will happen to their "personal relationship to God" if they act to reject mysticism. Although they agree with most that I have said about the dangers of a mystical theology, they still believe that their fellowship with God is a "personal" relationship. To reject these mystical, subjective attitudes is somehow to repudiate that relationship, thus hindering the Spirit's work in them. As a result, many Christians are unwilling to reject all mysticism. Unfortunately, mysticism tends to be so insidious that if we allow any room for it at all we soon find that it spreads its effects to many areas.

This poses a serious problem. If it is ever proper to call our relationship with God "personal," and if that means that the relationship is somehow mystical, then we must allow a major place for mysticism in our theology. If this is the case then much that has been said in this book is either clearly false or inadequate. But when is our relationship with God properly said to be "personal," and is it therefore mystical? When we answer these questions in the light of Scripture, I believe we will see that the fear expressed by my friends and other Christians is unjustified.

It may be surprising to some that nowhere in the Bible is a "personal relationship" commanded, recommended, or even mentioned. That is, the phrase *personal relationship*, or any synonym, is not found in Scripture. This, however, does not mean that the concept is not there. The biblical writers, for instance, did not use the word *Trinity* to describe God. The concept of the Trinity, however, is clearly taught in the Word.

The answer to our question depends upon what, exactly, we mean by the term *personal*. The Bible certainly does teach that as Christians we have a distinct relationship with God, one that is different from that which all other people have to Him. But in what sense can that relationship be called personal?

One explanation comes quickly to mind. God is personal. Each member of the Trinity is a Person. Because each human being is also a person, the relationship we have with our personal God is, therefore, that which exists between persons. I cannot have a personal relationship, in this sense, with a dog, since it is not a person. However, this is not the meaning of *personal* that concerns my friends. After all, the relationship between all men and God is equally personal in this sense.

Another possible meaning that Christians may intend by "personal relationship" is the conscious recognition of God's Personhood as we relate to Him. Not all men relate to Him like this. The atheist does not recognize God's existence at all. The pantheist sees Him as a force or thing, but not a Person. However, this still does not capture what most Christians seem to have in mind when they speak of a "personal relationship" with Christ. There are those non-Christians who acknowledge both God's existence and His Personhood. In spite of this, we would say that they do not have a "personal" relationship with God.

The Bible teaches that if we are God's children by faith, then we have the Holy Spirit living in us (1 Cor. 3:16; 6:19-20; Rom. 8:9). Thus, there exists a relationship between us and God that is closer than that between any two human beings. By *personal relationship* we acknowledge this very close, intimate relationship between us and the Spirit of God. Unfortunately, when Christian friends express their fear that a repudiation of mysticism is a repudiation of their personal relationship with God, their attention seems to be centered not on God's dwelling in them but on something else. This dimension which they treasure is something they feel, not something they know, nor even the reality of which they are aware. It seems they have in mind a subjective "something" they sense. For them, this inner feeling is essential to the relationship with God. To lack the feeling would prove that the relationship no longer exists.

RELATING TO GOD: EMOTIONS

Attention must focus at this point on the difference between emotions and mysticism. A rejection of mysticism is not the same as saying that feelings about God are to be rejected. Every important fact will produce certain emotions in us that are appropriate to that fact. This is emotional health. Having feelings is good and proper. This alone is not mysticism. Emotions become mystical when we begin to do something improper with them. When we make feelings the means of gaining knowledge, or when we make them a test of truth, or when we come to see them as the reality itself, then our emotions become misdirected. The repudiation of mysticism is not the denial of proper emotions. Instead, it is the assertion that reason, not emotion, is the tool for grasping and testing truth.

A personal relationship to God is possible because God, possessing divine Personhood, has created us persons, and He desires our closeness to Himself. The relationship itself consists of His residence within us as His temple. His purpose is to control us totally—body, soul, and spirit. Our minds, wills, and emotions are to be brought into total subjection to Him so that we will increasingly reflect the very nature of Christ (Rom. 8:29). For this purpose He created us and then saved us. As we have already seen, this does not free us from responsibility to manage our minds, our wills, and our bodies. We do not become automatons. Rather, we are freed to be what we were created for, to function properly, to be all God intended us to be.

Our relationship to Him is the closest possible. This is the fact. How we respond emotionally to this fact will depend on many things, such as the degree to which we understand this, our emotional temperament, the state of our physical health, and so forth. But the emotion per se is not the relationship, nor is the relationship dependent on the emotion.

The fear of Christian friends concerning the possible loss of their relationship with God results from at least three sources: either they wrongly identify the relationship with the emotion; or they are so enamored with their emotions that they will not allow anything to threaten those specific feelings; or they believe that the emotion is the infallible test of their relation to God. All three of these ideas violate biblical teaching. The idea that the emotion itself is the relationship means there is no real relation to God at all; our emotions are just one component of human personality, nothing more. The ideal that emotion is the proper and infallible test by which to determine that the proper relation to God exists, indicates a form of mysticism. These people are trusting their subjective inclinations, whereas the clear statements of God in Scripture should be sufficient.

The third idea controls people to whom emotions are very important—often much more important than facts. They cling to their emotions in a love embrace. They seem to think that the significance of their lives is totally bound up with their feelings, that all that really matters is how one feels. This is a form of sensuality, that is, an inordinate concern for and with the senses, in this case, with inner "senses" or feelings. Sensuality is itself not mysticism, but may easily lead to it. Sensuality in all forms is condemned in Scripture.

In much of what we have been discussing the problems arise from giving an improper importance to subjective states, urges, or impressions. In their proper perspective such feelings may be good and desirable. They may have a proper function, but that function is neither to provide information, nor to test truth. It is not wrong to feel an intimate closeness to God, but it is wrong to base our confidence of such a relationship solely on our feelings.

RELATING TO GOD: PRAYER

The role of prayer is another point of confusion for those who fear the loss of a personal relationship if they renounce mysticism. Some believe that a relationship with God can properly be personal only if there is a continuing two-way conversation between the persons involved. Thus, to have a personal relationship with God necessarily means that we speak to God in prayer about the various details of our daily lives, and He, in turn, responds in some direct manner. Since the Bible does not tell us what to do about diaper rash on the baby, a car that will not start, or buying a thousand shares of stock, Scripture alone is not seen as God's response to our part of the conversation. Therefore, according to this viewpoint, to have a personal relationship with God, God must respond in some direct manner. The principles revealed in the Bible and brought to our consciousness by the Spirit of God are deemed an inadequate response on God's part. Because most Christians do not expect to hear God speaking out loud to them in words, it seems natural to expect an inner impression as God's part of the conversation. Lacking these inner impressions, a person might doubt that he has the personal relationship to God that he should have. God is not talking to him.

This view, like the others we have examined, is confusing and mistaken. To avoid misunderstanding, we must be clear about the matter of prayer. Christians have the great privilege of bringing to God all the details of their daily lives—the diaper rashes, the mechanical breakdowns, the financial problems, and also the pleasure in the baby's first step, the comfort of a pleasant trip, and the business success. Our heavenly Father, the infinite, personal God of the universe, is interested in all the details of our lives. The problem, then, is not in speaking to God about these details. The difficulty results from expecting inner impressions as God's response.

This faulty view actually rests on the failure to understand just how intimate and close the relationship is between the Christian and his heavenly Father. People view God as an outsider speaking to our minds through our emotions. God is "out there," striving to communicate through a means that is inadequate and foreign to the process of normal communication.

However, God lives in us by His Holy Spirit. Therefore the picture of God trying to communicate to us from
"out there" is incorrect. God is in us. He is not in our
spirits distinct from our minds, as Watchman Nee teaches, but rather He is as much "in" our minds as in any
other part. He seeks to control every part of us. Thus His
response involves our minds. As we fill our minds with
His written Word, He uses that revelation to communicate His desires and wisdom to us.

We experience the Holy Spirit's work in us, not primarily as inner, totally subjective, noncognitive impressions, but as thoughts that are wise, just, loving, kind—in
other words, as godly, wise thinking about the issues of
life. We do not experience this as some other person ad-
dressing us, but rather as our minds influenced and directed by the Holy Spirit using the Scriptures.

There are, then, two factors constituting God's response to our prayers. God "speaks to us," first and fore-
most, through the propositional information found in the
Scriptures. The Bible is God's "letter" to us, His "instruc-
tion book," His verbal part of the conversation. We speak
to God in prayer; He speaks to us through His Word.

The second part involves His control of our entire
persons. It results in our wise thoughts, plans, and words.
This should not be seen as "our doing," in the sense that
we become proud of such wisdom. Where there is true
wisdom its source is always God, to whom all praise and
glory belongs. As we yield to Him, "we think God's
thoughts," because He is controlling our minds.

This may sound as though our thoughts are somehow trustworthy or, on the other hand, that we are not
responsible for them. I am not advocating either of these
positions. As sinful, fallen beings we are capable of great
error and wickedness. However, as redeemed children of
God we have the Holy Spirit who uses our minds. Our
thoughts, intentions, plans, and words must always be

measured against the Word of God. Applying that standard requires our minds.

Our personal relationship with God is a fact based on God's doing, not on ours. The fear that to reject mysticism is somehow to reject or to endanger that relationship rests on confusion concerning what it means to be a Christian. If the relationship one has with God is actually a mystical thing, then it is not scriptural; it does not really exist. In that case, to believe that it does exist is a false belief. It would be well if we were rid of it. Losing a false "personal relationship" is not something to be feared. The true relationship we have with God is in no way endangered by ridding ourselves of mysticism.

RELATING TO GOD: THE SPIRIT

How, then, are we to make effective the Holy Spirit's ministry in our lives, if no mystical elements are allowable? Such a question implies that somehow, as Christians, we must do something to make effective the Holy Spirit's work in us. It is not uncommon to hear sermons that maintain that our efforts are indispensable to seeing God's purposes carried out in our lives. We must pray for the Spirit's work, we must "appropriate" His ministry, we must unlock His power, we are told.

There are difficulties involved in thinking about God in the above-mentioned way, even though there is some truth in it. It implies that He is either reluctant to do His work in us, or else that He responds only to the correct formula. A formula approach seems appropriate only if the Holy Spirit is merely a force controlled by certain "laws." The formula is the way in which these "laws" are activated so that His power is made available, as in the case of atomic energy. However, the Holy Spirit is a Person, as are the other members of the Trinity, and He chooses to do His work in us. The Scripture gives us no formula for releasing His power in our lives. However, it does indicate that there are conditions which allow Him to work, and others which prevent His effectual working. We are told to *walk in the Spirit* (Gal. 5:16), *grieve not the Spirit* (Eph. 4:30), and *quench not the Spirit* (1 Thess. 5:19). But these directives do not constitute a formula that somehow guarantees the Spirit's action in one's life. His activity and power are under His sovereign control.

Many Christian friends who speak of human conditions in relating to the Spirit know full well that the Holy Spirit is a Person and He operates as a personal being. They do not believe He is reluctant to do His work in their lives. When pressed, they might, nevertheless, express a certain frustration that many evangelical Christians feel. "Why, then," they might ask, "is it that God seems to be doing such great things in the lives of many others, but I don't see the same thing in my life? How do I come to experience His ministry?"

Such a question suggests several problems, among them the thought that God is not doing for me what He is doing for others. Furthermore, there is something I must do to free Him to do what He wishes to accomplish in me. Both these suggestions contain degrees of truth, and potential for misunderstanding, as well.

We must, of course, recognize that unconfessed sin prevents the Spirit from doing for and in us all that He desires. For the sake of this discussion, however, let us assume that there is no unconfessed sin.

In grappling with these difficulties, we must remember that God is sovereign and that He does not intend that each of us fulfill the same role in life. Elijah was a man with a nature like ours, we are told (James 5:17), yet God has not given to any of us the precise role to play that He assigned to Elijah. Therefore, none of us experiences the ministry and power of the Holy Spirit in exactly the same way as Elijah experienced it. The same may be said about the apostles. We do not duplicate in our lives the work of God that they had. Those who suggest that we should do so may be forgetting the sovereignty of God. He has sovereignly made each of us special, has given us a special role in life, and has promised to empower us for just that role. Consequently, I should not necessarily expect to experience the work of the Holy Spirit in the same way as others do.

People often falsely believe that a Christian who is in proper fellowship with God faces no struggles and that part of the Holy Spirit's ministry is to make the Christian life an effortless one. Because of these false ideas, Christian testimonies and biographies tend to ignore real struggles. Consequently, our own struggles lead us to believe that we are not experiencing the Holy Spirit's work to the same degree as those whose glowing testimonies we hear or read about.

What of the related problem that suggests there is something *I* must do to "release" the power of the Spirit? Is that true? Understood in one way it certainly is correct. However, what many people mean by such statements is not true.

The relevant biblical command is "Be filled with the Spirit" (Eph. 5:18). In the parallel passage in Col. 3, Paul states basically the same thing in these words: "Let the word of Christ dwell in you richly" (v. 16). Earlier, in verse 2 of the same chapter he has commanded us to "set (our) affections on things above, not on things on the earth." We are to do something, but that something has to do with our attitude, our attention, and our knowledge. We are to fill our minds with the Word of God; we are consciously to value and love the things of God above those things that are part of this present world order. This demands an act of the will—a deliberate, moment-by-moment attitude that seeks to adopt God's perspective in all things. To do this, we must know His viewpoint.

Being filled with the Spirit (that is, having our entire being permeated by and controlled by the Spirit) is the direct result of allowing the Word of God to dwell in us richly.

Again we see the contrast between a proper biblical perspective and a mystical one. In an understanding dominated by mysticism, "being filled with the Spirit" is seen as an ecstatic experience of limited duration, having no direct, necessary relation to any intellectual grasp of the Scripture. Yet the biblical command is "to be being continually filled" (Greek verb present tense, Eph. 5:18), something that can never be true of an ecstatic state. Spirit-filling is to be a continuing condition that is related to the growing knowledge of the Word. In regard to the Bible's role, let us remember that it is not merely the ability to recall correctly the statements of Scripture. The Word is to "dwell in us," and it is to do so "richly." It is to permeate us. We are to understand it and be committed to it. We are to believe it, obey it, value it. It is to control our thoughts and shape our choices. It is to be our guide in all areas of life.

How does the ministry of the Holy Spirit become an actual reality in the life of the believer? He does His work in us and through us according to His sovereign plan. Our part is to allow Him to do His work by being filled with the Word. If we know and believe His Word we will realize that He is doing His work in us, even when we see nothing unusual happening.

Still, some might respond, "Is there no sense in which we are ever to be conscious of the Spirit's work in a more intimate, direct, momentary way?"

There certainly may be such moments. Some of them will be "positive" experiences; some of them may be quite unpleasant. For example, a well-developed, correctly taught conscience is a ready tool of the Holy Spirit. So is our mind, our memory—every part of us. To experience conviction of sin through conscience, while vitally important, is not a pleasant experience. What can be more "conscious" and intimate to us than the experiences of thought and conscience?

Summary and Conclusion

There may still be some who, failing to grasp how close the relation between God and His children is, will feel cheated if they do not have some subjective experience they can identify as the unique work of the Spirit. This yearning for the emotional element is likely the result of a history of mystically influenced teaching. It cannot be justified on scriptural ground. Tragically, this desire for feelings is also a strong temptation to mysticism itself.

CONCLUSION

What, then, are we to say to these things? If the arguments of this book are correct, mysticism is to be rejected wherever it is found. We must do so if we are to be true to the Scriptures and to our name as Christians and evangelicals. Why is this so?

As evangelical Christians we are bound by Scripture. It, and it alone, is our final criterion of truth. That which deviates from the Word of God is shown by that deviation to be false. Mysticism is such a deviation, both by its claim to provide a method for knowing God that is not the biblical way and by leading to theological claims that deviate from clear scriptural teaching.

Furthermore, there is another serious result from the mystical approach. To adopt mysticism as a legitimate way of approaching God is to reject the basis of the Protestant Reformation and the basis of evangelicalism. These foundations affirm that, apart from the knowledge that can be gained from God's created order, the Scriptures alone are the basis for all our knowledge of God. On the other hand, the mystic insists that there is another way, a better and "purer" way, of approaching God and gaining knowledge of Him. This is a rejection of the heart of Protestantism.

Finally, mysticism must be rejected because of its constant threat to biblical theology. Due to its very nature, it is a "way to gain knowledge" that prevents any effective check from an objective source. It tends to pervert any attempted test of its truthfulness. The strong temptation is to make mystical experience the basis for determining the meaning of the very Scriptures that otherwise might serve to stand in judgment against mysticism. Thus, the mystic uses his experience to determine the meaning of Scripture, instead of using Scripture to judge his experience. As a result, mystical experience is a constant source of false doctrine.

This tendency is not something new today. Even the medieval Roman Catholic mystics faced the problem. If one reads church history and the writings of the mystics he will see that those people were in almost constant trouble with the Catholic church. A major part of the conflict resulted from the difficulty they had in interpreting their mystical experiences in such a way that they did not conflict with established theology. The conflict raged even though the theological context of those times provided an opportunity for mysticism in a way that evangelicalism cannot ever do. The Catholic church had allowed into its authority-concepts the possibility of continued direct revelation. The evangelical categorically rules this out. Furthermore, without resting on Scripture alone there is no constraint for using the mind alone for knowledge. Therefore, the medieval Catholic church had opened the possibility that knowledge could occur through nonrational means. Such a possibility was closed in the Protestant Reformation by the *sola scriptura* principle. If the Reformers were being true to the Scriptures when they stated this principle, then permitting the possibility of truth through mysticism must be rejected as a violation of Scripture.

In view of all this, it seems strange that mysticism should have gained such a respected place in evangelical circles today. This has come about partly because it has not been recognized as mysticism. The influence of such movements as Pietism, which were often deeply mystical, but had some legitimate elements in them, may also have contributed to our insensitivity. Whatever the reasons for our present condition, we now face situations that are grave, subtle, and dangerous.

Dangers for Christians are magnified by the fact that we live in an age when mysticism is rapidly gaining favor in secular society. Because secular mysticism is popular, a "Christianized" mysticism is more attractive than is true Christianity to the world we are trying to reach. This is the appeal inherent in the charismatic movement—an appeal more from mysticism than from the gospel. It attracts adherents because it condones and encourages the very sensuality that the Bible condemns, although it hides this fact under the guise of Christianity. This is a form of apostasy.

To make matters worse, as such movements grow and become more respectable, Christians will tend to become less and less sensitive to the dangers of mysticism. At the same time, the influence of mystical ideas will increase, with the accompanying impact on Christian theology and the reduced resistance to mystical heresy.

It is high time that the evangelical community awoke to the dangerous influences we have been harboring in our midst. If we are to be effective in presenting a clear picture of the gospel, of the nature of our God and Father, and of His expectations for mankind, we must rid ourselves of this counterfeit spirituality that Satan has so subtly developed in the church. Unless we are able to do so, we will fail to obey the biblical command to "be on guard for yourselves and for all the flock" (Acts 20:28). May the Father of Mercy grant us the vision and courage to purify His church.

SELECTIVE BIBLIOGRAPHY

Pro-mysticism Literature

Foster, Richard J. *Celebration of Discipline.* New York: Harper & Row, 1978.
    In an attempt to provide practical advice on living the Christian life, Foster promotes a very mystical view of Christianity. He acknowledges his debt to such mystics as George Fox, Francis of Assisi, Evelyn Underhill, Thomas Merton, Madam Guyon, and others; and the result is a position similiar to that found in the Medieval Catholic church. Much of what the Protestant Reformers opposed is promoted by Foster.

Inge, William Ralph. *Mysticism in Religion.* Westport, Conn.: Greenwood, 1948.
    Inge was formerly Dean of St. Paul's. He strongly promotes mysticism, believing it to be the only available substitute to the Bible, which he rejects as unreliable and discredited.

James, William. *The Varieties of Religious Experience.* New York: Collier Macmillan, 1961.
James, often called 'the father of modern psychology,' examines the psychology involved in various religious experiences, including mystical ones. Very favorably inclined toward mysticism.

LaShan, Lawrence. *The Medium, the Mystic, and the Physicist.* New York: Ballantine, 1974.
LaShan argues that in order to understand certain theories in modern physics one must adopt the same metaphysical position that mediums and mystics hold when they are in their trance states. It appears he wishes to transfer the intellectual respectability accorded by our society to science to spiritist mediumship and mysticism.

Mitchell, Edgar D. *Psychic Exploration.* New York: G. P. Putnam's, 1974.
The book states that it ". . . attempts to provide an authoritative encyclopedic volumn on psychic research." Describes the scientific exploration of "paranormal" events. Helps the reader see how close the relationship between mysticism and occultism can be.

Nee, Watchman. *The Release of the Spirit.* Cloverdale, Ind.: Ministry of Life, 1965.
Nee argues that the spirit of man, which he defines as totally intuitive and nonrational, must dominate man. The soul, defined as mind, emotions, and will, must be "broken" to release the spirit so that God may do His work. Presents a very mystical view of Christianity.

————. *The Spiritual Man.* New York: Christian Fellowship Publishers, 1977.
Presents Nee's position in its most complete and systematic form. Develops his mystical view of man and argues that one who is not mystical is not a Christian. Seems to have been a major influence on the charismatic movement.

Underhill, Evelyn. *Practical Mysticism*. New York: E. P. Dutton, 1943.

Underhill's writings are considered modern classics in the description, defense, and promotion of mysticism. Her definition of mysticism exhibits some of the ambiguity inherent in the subject.

Anti-mysticism Literature

Clark, Gordon H. *Faith and Saving Faith*. Jefferson, Md.: The Trinity Foundation, 1983.

Among other things, Clark shows that faith is not a feeling, an intuitive urge, or a mystical category, but rather is a rational function.

Duddy, Neil T., and the SCP. *The God-Men*. Downers Grove, Ill.: InterVarsity, 1981.

This book provides examples of the implications of mystical theology, especially the implications of Watchman Nee's position.

Friesen, Garry. *Decision Making & the Will of God*. Portland, Oreg.: Multnomah, 1980.

A very careful, thorough treatment of the biblical position on decision making. Shows that the Bible does not teach that God guides through mystical means.

Hunt, Dave, and McMahon, T. A. *The Seduction of Christianity*. Eugene, Oreg.: Harvest House, 1985.

Exposes the growing influence of occult beliefs and practices within the church. Hunt is specific in identifying people and movements. Shows the relation of mystical philosophies and practices to many contemporary religious movements.

MacArthur, John F., Jr. *The Charismatics*. Grand Rapids, Mich.: Zondervan, 1978.
A good examination of many of the theological issues that distinguish charismatics from other Christians. Although MacArthur does not deal directly with mysticism, what he indicates is that the biblical position speaks strongly against it.

Macaulay, Ranald, and Barrs, Jerram. *Being Human*. Downers Grove, Ill.: InterVarsity, 1978.
Presents an excellent picture of the biblical teaching on what it means to be spiritual. In the process, the authors show that true spirituality is not mystical.

Russell, Bertrand. *Mysticism and Logic*. London: George Allen & Unwin, 1970.
Although not predominantly anti-mystical, this book provides some interesting and useful analysis of what constitutes mysticism. Russell, a famous atheist, tends to reject mysticism in favor of scientific naturalism.

Moody Press, a ministry of the Moody Bible Institute, is designed for education, evangelization, and edification. If we may assist you in knowing more about Christ and the Christian life, please write us without obligation: Moody Press, c/0 MLM, Chicago, Illinois 60610